Reinaldo Domingos

Money Boy
Goes to school

1st Edition

About the series

The series "Money Boy" is a children's adaptation based upon the DSOP Financial Education Methodology, conceived by master, professor, educator, and financial therapist Reinaldo Domingos.

The series is part of the DSOP Financial Education Program that ranges from grammar school to college. It consists of 30 didactic volumes (15 textbooks and 15 teacher's books) and six paradidactic volumes that comprise subjects of family, diversity, sustainability, autonomy, and citizenship.

In addition to the books, the schools that adopt the DSOP Financial Education Program are entitled to pedagogical training, financial education workshops for teachers, lectures for the students and the community, and access to the school website (portalescolas.dsop.com.br), which consists of class plans, interactive activities (games), videos, and exclusive access to students, teachers, parents, and school managers.

For further information, please visit www.dsop.com.br/escolas or contact a local franchisee in your area by searching on our website www.dsop.com.br/franquia.

What's happening

After learning important lessons from his mother during childhood, this captivating character now faces a world of new challenges at school.

In this new environment, Ray encounters people and situations, which become essential to his knowledge and development.

He meets Spender; Constance, the classroom teacher; and Mr. Raymoney, the intriguing math teacher.

Despite some unpleasant experiences at first, the boy maintains his courage, innocence, and determination to overcome obstacles, along with the support of his mother. He knows he can count on his math teacher to reveal the "magic of money"—the four steps of the DSOP Methodology.

By coming into contact with this promising world of financial education, the boy ends up involving the whole family, promoting several changes, and fulfilling many short and long dreams.

© Editora DSOP, 2016
© Reinaldo Domingos, 2015

President
Reinaldo Domingos

Text editor
Renata de Sá
Samir Thomaz

Art editor
Joyce Thomaz

Illustrator
Ariel Fajtlowicz

Editorial producer
Amanda Torres

English language version
Joan Rumph
Milena Cavichiolo

All rights reserved to Editora DSOP
Av. Paulista, 726 - Cj. 1210 - Bela Vista
ZIP Code: 01310-910 - Brazil - São Paulo - SP
Phone: 55 11 3177-7800
www.editoradsop.com.br

Dados Internacionais de Catalogação na Publicação (CIP)
(Câmara Brasileira do Livro, SP, Brasil)

```
Domingos, Reinaldo
    Money boy : goes to school / Reinaldo Domingos ;
illustrations Ariel Fajtlowicz ; [translation
Joan Rumph e Milena Cavichiolo]. -- São Paulo :
Editora DSOP, 2015.

    Título original: O menino do dinheiro : vai à
escola
    ISBN 978-85-8276-142-7


    1. Dinheiro - Literatura infantojuvenil
2. Finanças - Literatura infantojuvenil
I. Fajtlowicz, Ariel. II. Título.


15-07572                                    CDD-028.5
```

Índices para catálogo sistemático:

1. Educação financeira : Literatura infantil
   028.5
2. Educação financeira : Literatura infantojuvenil
   028.5

Contents

New year, new life.. 7
Learning how to count... 13
The fabulous math teacher..................................... 17
A good lesson... 23
A big mess.. 27
The lie... 31
The following day.. 37
Lies don't travel far... 41
Moment of truth.. 45
Good news... 51
A couple of surprises.. 55
The treasure map.. 61
First lessons... 67
Diagnose... 73
Family that thinks together.................................... 79
Dreaming.. 83
Son's dreams and father's dreams....................... 87
Budgeting... 91
The big secret.. 97
Saving... 101
A dream never dreamt... 109

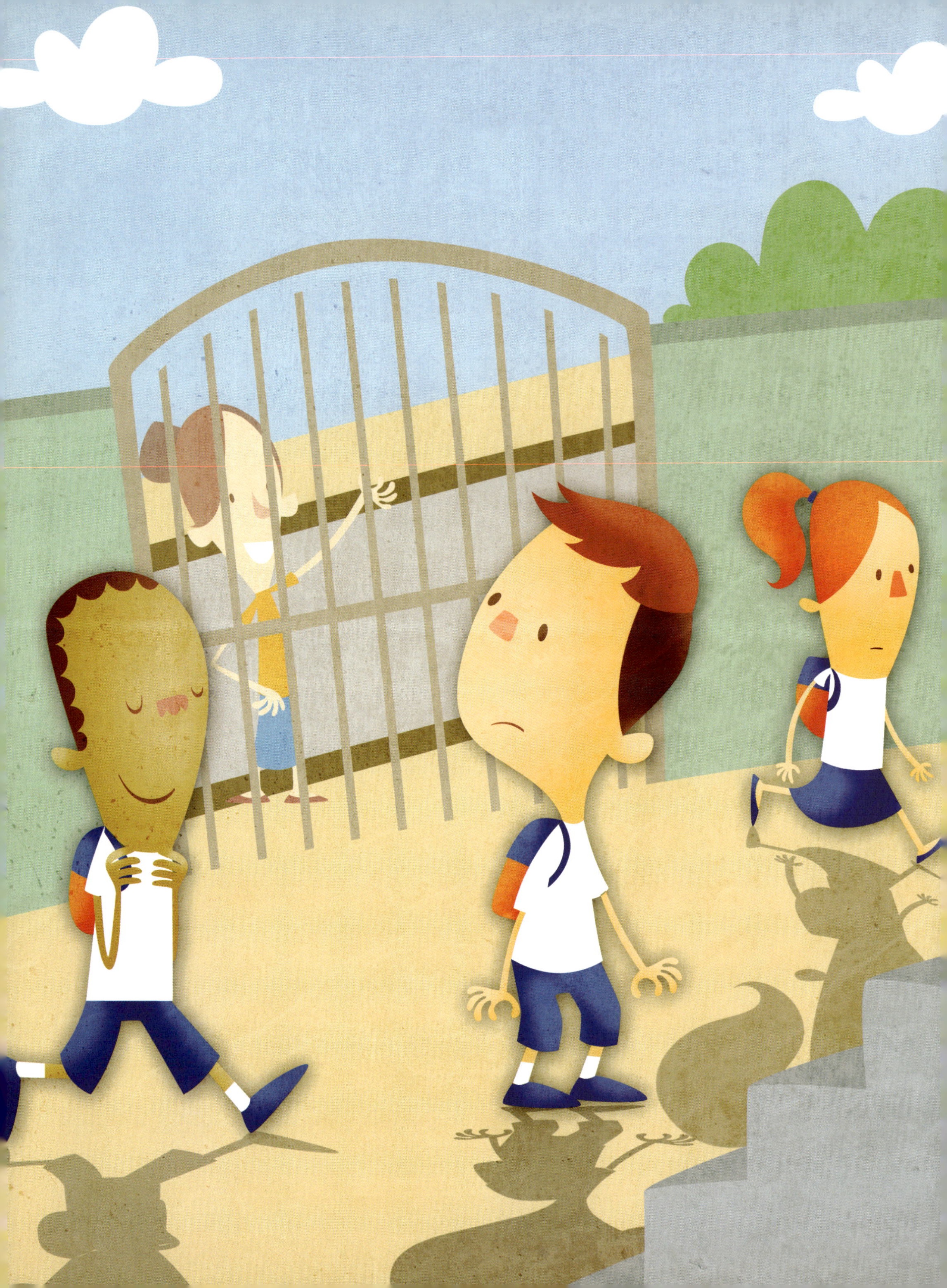

New year, new life

Time flew by in the small town of Lagoa Branca. Another year had begun, bringing everyone the promise of good news.

At Money Boy's home, the family routine had not changed. Mrs. Foresight took care of the house, the orchard, family meals and, whenever she had some free time, she sold her cosmetics and jewelry. Mr. Unaware, as usual, returned home tired and quiet.

Money Boy's heart filled with excitement, as he marked off each calendar day until his first day of school. At night, the anticipation and fear of the unknown kept him from falling asleep, and he nervously rolled over in bed from side to side.

When the day finally came, he could barely wait for his mother to fix breakfast. He showed up in the kitchen proudly wearing his school uniform, carrying his backpack.

Upon arriving at school, everything seemed new and scary. The hardest part came when the huge school gate closed and his mother remained outside, waving at him.

Up to that day, the boy had never been without his mother around. He thought he would really miss her, but it was not quite like that.

Soon he realized other children were having their first day of school as well, so he put on a brave face. *If they can make it, I can make it, too!*

And so he did, with the help of his teacher, Mrs. Constance, who was a very kind and gentle lady. She wore her long, straight hair tied back in a ponytail.

Mrs. Constance had prepared a special lesson to welcome the students on their first day. They drew, painted, and played with clay. The boy liked all those new things, but what he became fascinated with the most were the stories Mrs. Constance told, imitating the characters with funny faces.

The boy was not used to hearing stories read aloud from books. His parents didn't read much at home. The only stories he knew were a few folk legends his mother told to him and the adventures of a TV hero.

He really enjoyed listening to the fairy tales so much that he didn't even notice how much time had passed. He only realized it when the bell rang.

On their walk back home Mrs. Foresight asked, "So, how was your first day of school?"

Money Boy described all the exciting events of the day. "It was all very cool, but I still haven't learned any of the things I wanted to learn," he said.

"What exactly are these things you're so anxious to learn, son?"

"You told me I would learn more about piggy banks and coins, but the teacher didn't even mention them."

In a calm voice, Mrs. Foresight said, "Son, be patient. Today was your first day at school. Remember what I always say, everything has its own time."

"But when is that time going to come, mom?"

"I believe it's when you begin your mathematics lessons."

"Ma what?"

"Mathematics, son. Math is the science of numbers," she replied. "But you're still too young. You first need to get used to school and to your schedule. Next year, you will be taking your first math lessons."

"Only next year? Then why do I have to go to school this year if the one thing I want to learn is not going to happen until next year?" he said with a sigh.

"It happens that there are many other important things you need to learn besides math, young boy! In the meantime, what is important is that you are at school now. The rest, time will take care of it."

As always, Mrs. Foresight was right. The boy did learn some interesting things throughout that year. However, the teacher stressed that the most important lesson was getting to know new people and learning to respect their space and time. The boy learned those things quickly.

Money Boy loved to talk and whenever he had the opportunity, he would always ask people if they had a piggy bank. At first, everybody found that to be a weird question and then he would explain.

"I have three piggy banks. Every year, my mother buys me a new one. I even gave one to my dad as a gift!" he said, grinning.

Sometimes his friends would get annoyed and think he was bragging about himself, just like those kids that keep repeating, "I have it and you don't!"

But as Money Boy continued to explain, everybody realized it was nothing like that.

"My mother taught me that, if we learn early in life to save some of the coins that pass through our hands, we can make our dreams come true. Already, I have purchased a soccer ball and a toy car with the coins I saved."

Some kids got jealous when they heard the boy talking like that. Sometimes they even picked on him.

However, most of the time, they thought he was right.

Money Boy - Goes to school

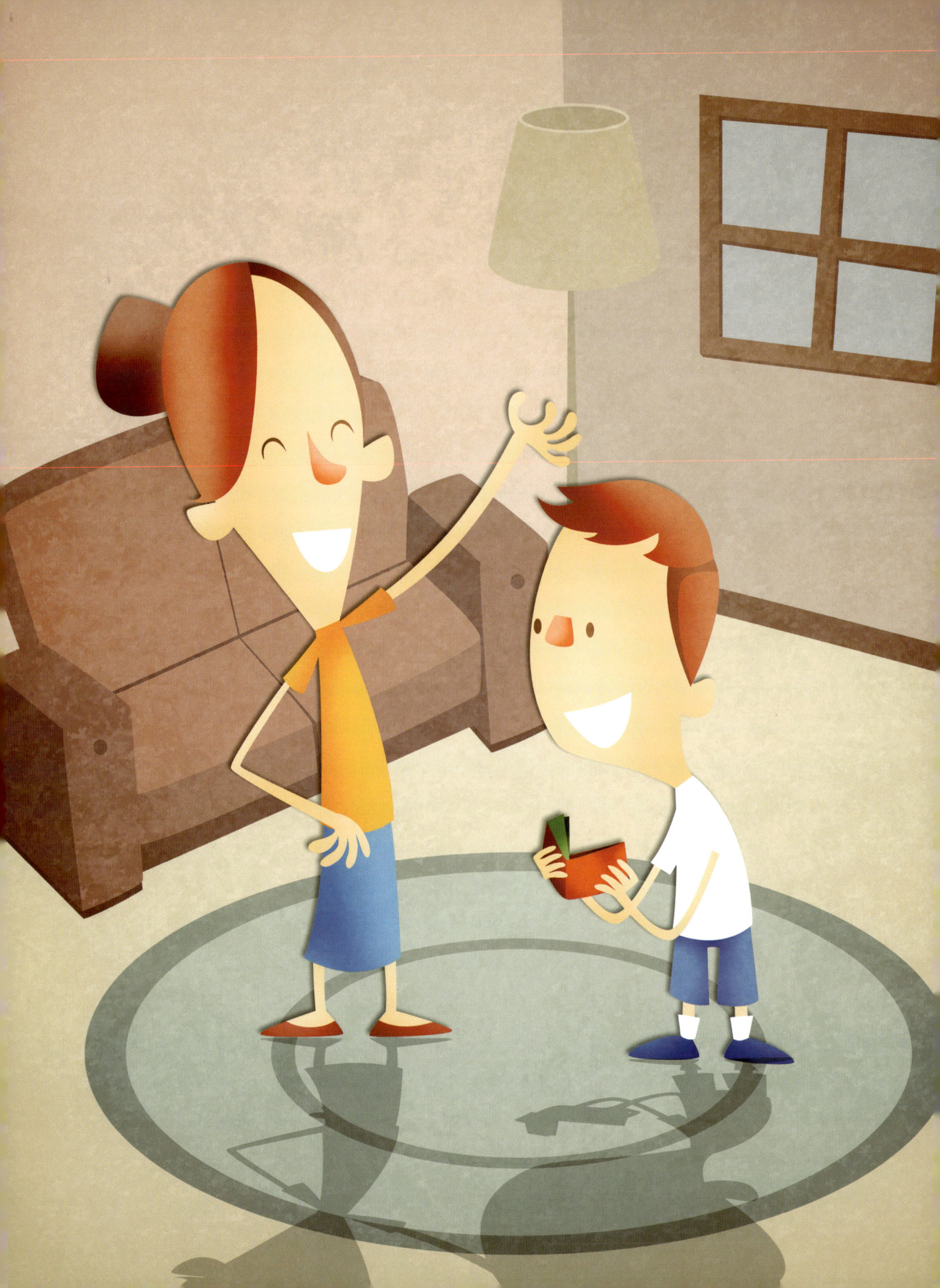

Learning how to count

Throughout the first school year—besides playing with clay, drawing, and gluing papers—Money Boy learned the alphabet and how to count from 1 to 100. He quickly recited all the numbers in a row without making any mistakes.

Mrs. Foresight closely followed her son's progress.

"You see how important your first year is? The things you're learning now are the foundation for learning the basic mathematical operations: adding, subtracting, multiplying and dividing," she said.

The boy didn't exactly know what "basic mathematical operations" were, but he knew he was good with numbers, and he really liked that. Every day after school, he showed his mother what he had learned, walking on the sidewalk and counting to 100 several times along the way.

At the end of school vacation and right before classes would start, Money Boy turned seven years old. That meant it was time to open his third piggy bank.

This time Money Boy helped his mother count the coins, as he already mastered counting from 1 to 100. He created all the piles of coins by himself.

Mrs. Foresight told him the amount of money saved was even larger than the previous times. Indeed it was. There were 29 piles of coins, much more than the 19 piles he counted the last time.

"Are you paying attention, son? The more you save the more money you get!"

"This time I'm not buying anything," Money Boy said. "I just want to give daddy some extra coins, because his piggy bank is taking a long time to fill up. The rest of the money I'm going to save again in another piggy."

"Then we will have to buy two new piggy banks. One to save the coins you already have and another one for additional coins you are going to save. I have a better idea," said the mother, giving the boy another package.

The boy tore open the paper to discover a wallet with room for coins and bills. Before he could ask anything, Mrs. Foresight began to explain.

"From now on, with the money you have, you'll be able to replace your coins with bills just like the ones my customers pay me with. Soon you will be learning at school about how much each bill is worth. For now let's just stop by the bank so you can exchange your coins for bills," said the mother, dropping all the coins inside a plastic bag.

The heavy bag of coins impressed the bank clerk. While she was counting them, the clerk told Mrs. Foresight, "This boy will go far in life! He sure is smart!"

For every pile of 5¢, 10¢, and 25¢ coins, the bank clerk handed the boy a certain amount of paper money called dollar bills. Money Boy's new wallet now contained crisp dollar bills. He even received some change back, because there were not enough coins to exchange for a dollar bill.

Despite the large number of coins he exchanged at the bank, the boy considered the amount too little.

Mrs. Foresight explained, "Some bills are worth much more than all those coins put together. It's something you'll understand better with time. I'm sure your school will be teaching you more about money."

On their way back home, Money Boy carefully studied the pictures on the dollar bills, the numbers shown on each side, and slowly read the words printed on them.

Since he had begun to read, he wanted to understand everything and identify all the words. Sometimes he grew impatient. In his mind, he still remembered his mother's old saying, "Everything in its own time."

At night, the boy dreamed about all the things he still needed to learn and wished for the classes to start again soon.

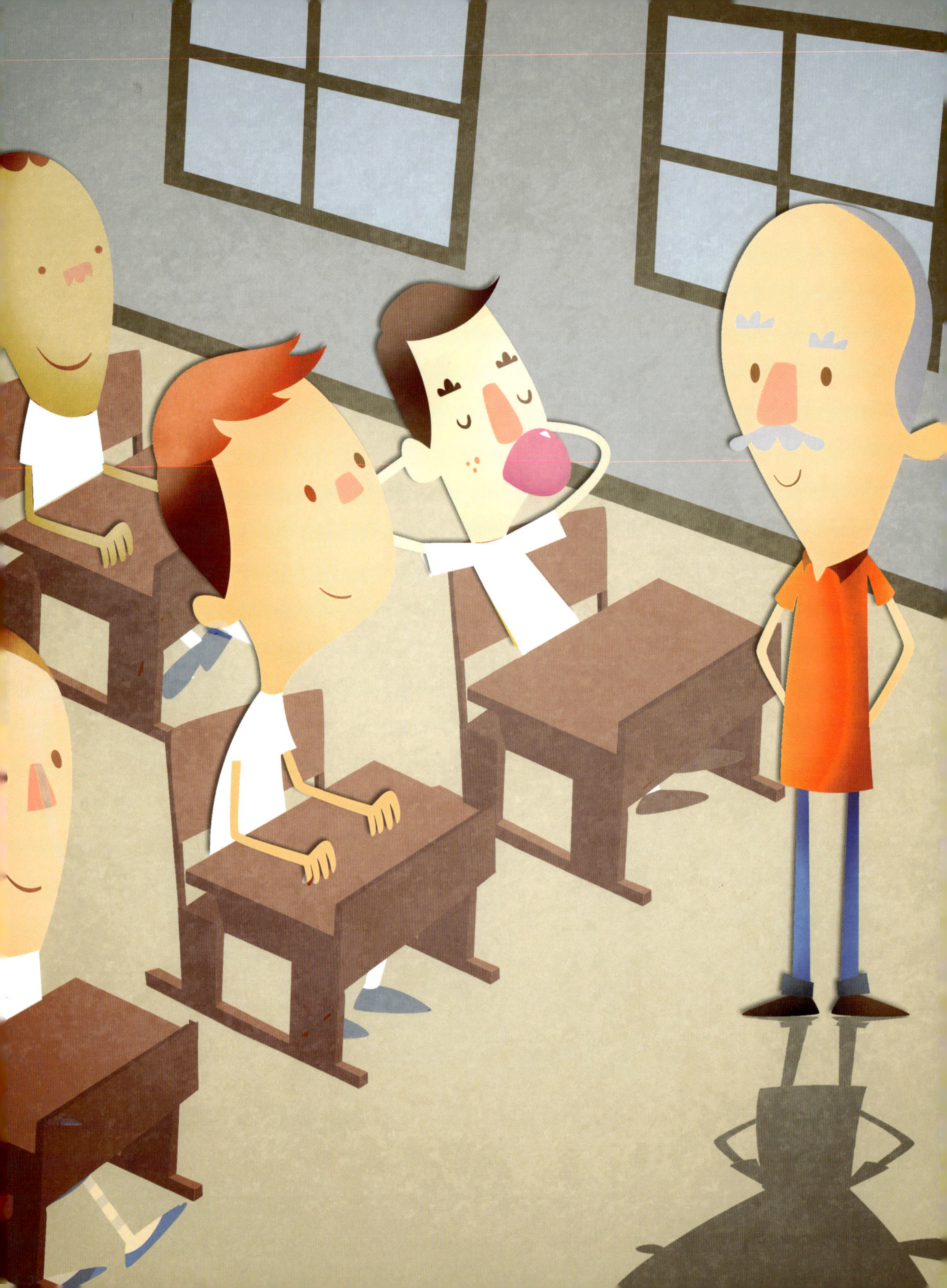

The fabulous math teacher

The beginning of the school year came at last, as slowly as the trains arriving fully loaded at the station. This year, Money Boy would learn and experience many new things. On his first day, his mother said, "This is the last time I will walk with you to school. From now on, you will have to go by yourself."

At first, the boy became quite anxious for his house was kind of far from school. Then he saw many other children also walking to school alone. He left his fear behind and started to think it would be a good thing to have the freedom to be on his own.

Another new and more important experience was meeting his math teacher, Mr. Raymond. Mrs. Constance was still head of the class and taught history, geography, and science. Mr. Raymond would teach English and math.

Mr. Raymond was a friendly person with a huge smile. It came as a big surprise to Money Boy that he and his teacher shared the same name.

His mother had chosen the name, Raymond, because it meant something like "born to rule," and she wanted her son to become a real leader.

The boy sat in the classroom thinking about that, when Mr. Raymond began asking the name of each student. When his turn came, he said his name was Money Boy and the teacher looked intrigued.

"So, look who's here! Then you're the famous Money Boy?" asked Mr. Raymond, coming closer to the boy seated in the front row.

The boy felt uneasy and stuttered a little bit.

"I mean my real name is also Raymond, just like yours, but everybody calls me Money Boy."

The teacher raised his eyebrows. He was silent for a moment and then said, "Wow, what a coincidence! So you're twice my namesake," tapping lightly on the head of the boy, who didn't know the meaning of the word, namesake.

Mr. Raymond noticed the puzzled looks from the other students, too, as he walked toward the front of the room. He sat on top of his desk and began speaking, swinging his legs, exactly like children do when sitting in tall chairs.

"Namesake is when we have the same name as another person," Mr. Raymond began to explain. "Money Boy is twice that in relation to me, because my name is also Raymond, and I have a nickname that's close to his. My father gave me a nickname when I was a kid. My nickname is Raymoney."

"Raymoney?" the students repeated, laughing.

"Exactly!" said the teacher walking toward the whiteboard, where he wrote his nickname in large letters: RAYMONEY

"And what does Raymoney mean?" asked Spender, a red-haired kid, sitting beside the boy in the front row.

"Well, it's a synonym for money, of course. My father created that nickname for me because he thought I would become a sort of money master when I grew up," the teacher replied, sitting down at his desk.

"I don't believe that," whispered Spender, popping a huge bubble with his chewing gum. "Now, besides Money Boy, we also have Raymoney!"

Mr. Raymoney, who was always aware of everything that happened inside the classroom, spoke up. "Well Spender, I believe your classmate and I might have something in common to teach you."

The kid shook his shoulders, stuck his hand in his pocket, and pulled out a bunch of fresh bubble gum. He chose a couple pieces and shoved them into his mouth.

Mr. Raymoney went on with the story and told the class his father had given him that nickname because he wanted him to be a prosperous guy.

Then he asked the class if anyone knew what it meant to be a prosperous person, but everybody remained silent. The teacher wrote the word "prosperous" on the board and explained that a prosperous person was a wealthy person.

Spender, in a mocking tone, shouted out, "You mean rich? If that's it, I think your father failed, because I don't know of any rich teacher."

"That's precisely why you're wrong, Spender. One can be rich even though he or she doesn't earn that much money, or be poor having a fortune."

Then the teacher began to write something else on the board, but the bell rang before he could finish. He told the students they would solve a problem together right after the break.

Money Boy remained seated for a while thinking about the things the teacher had just told the class. Spender passed by and teased him, "What's up, Money Boy, aren't you buying anything today? How come our mathematician doesn't have a single penny to buy candy with?"

Money Boy couldn't answer fast enough before Spender raced out of the room. The teacher saw the look of anger on Money Boy's face and told him, "Never mind. After the break, we'll solve that other problem, too."

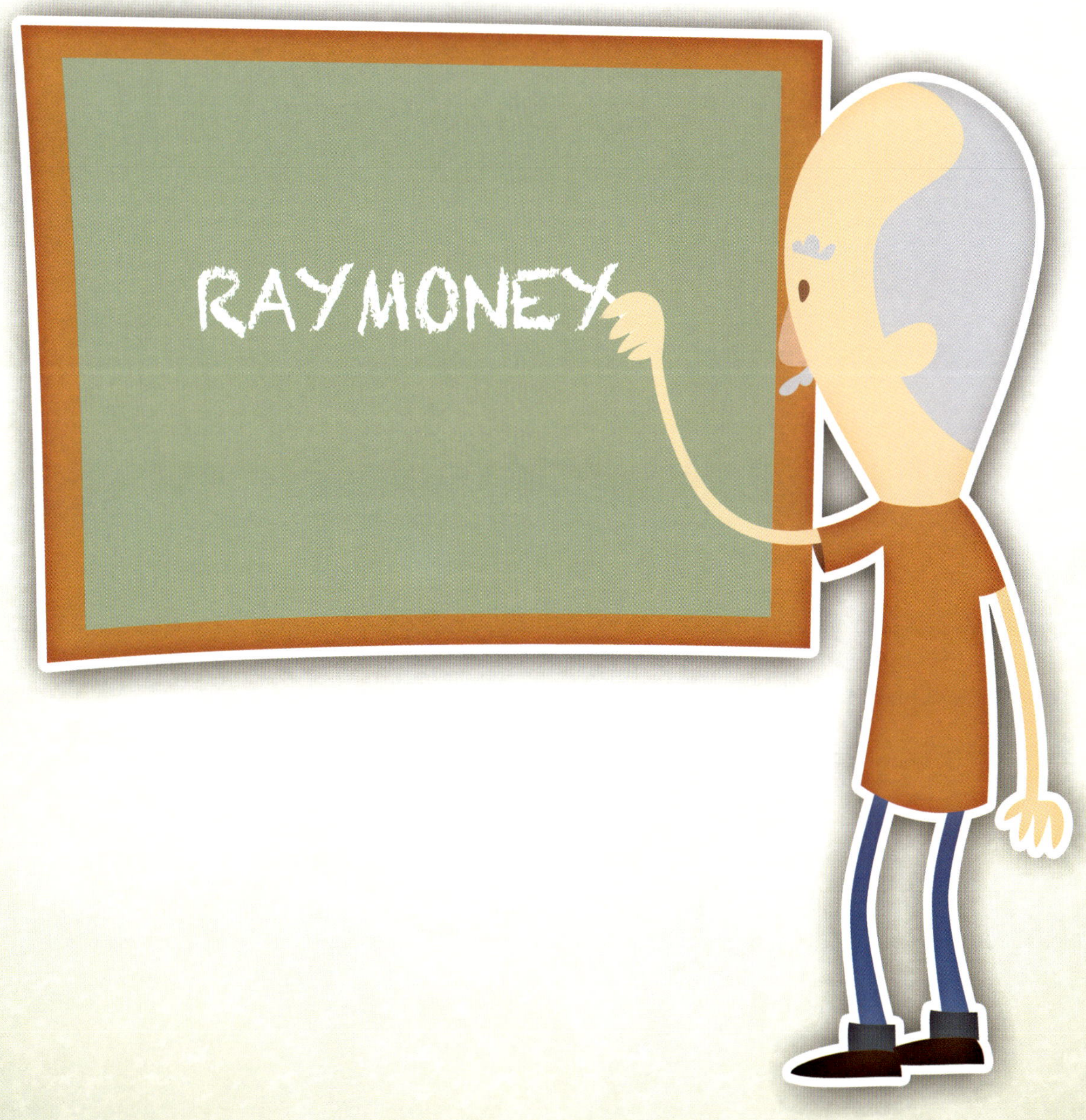
RAYMONEY

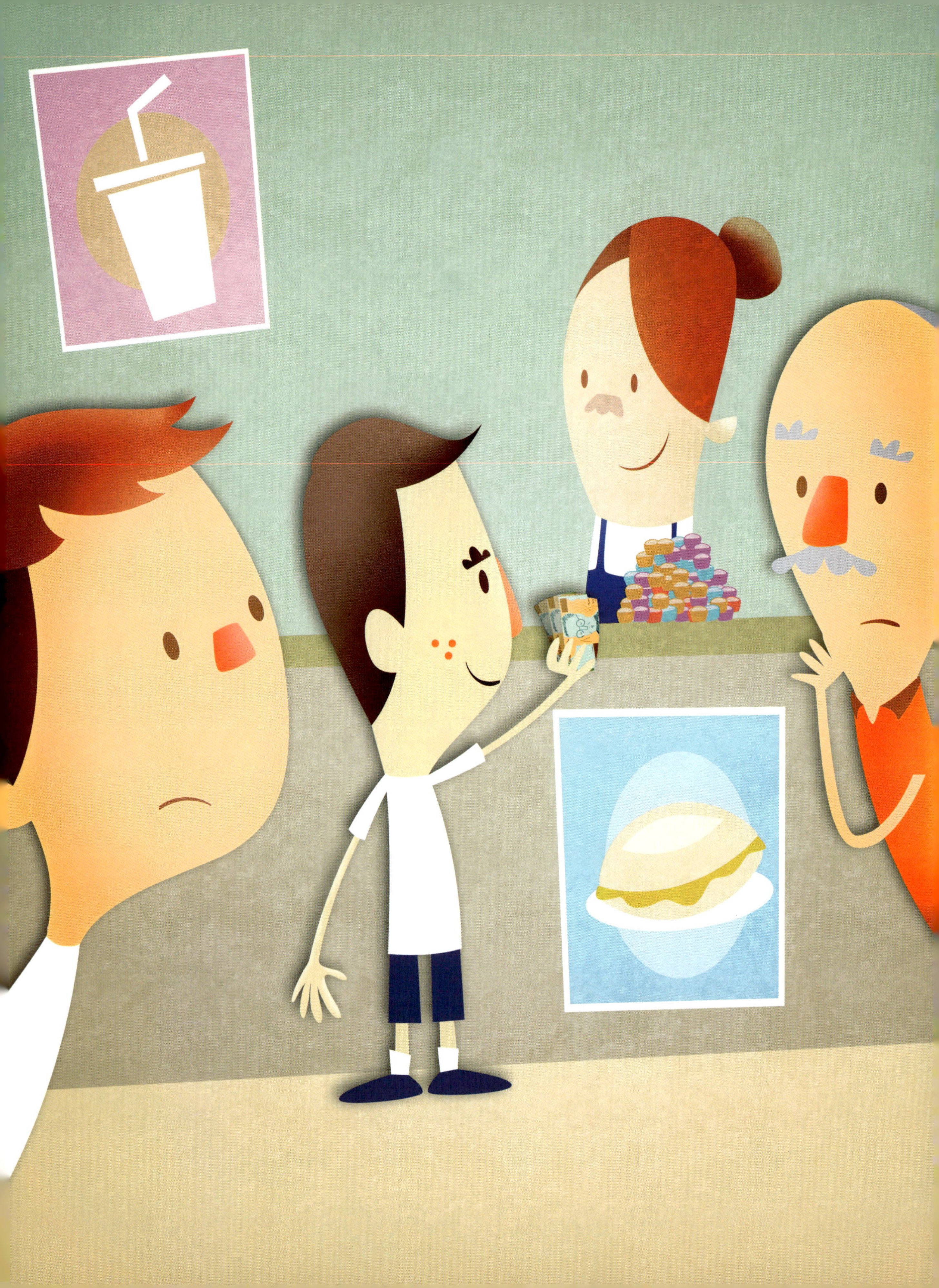

A good lesson

During the break, Mr. Raymoney saw the way Spender emptied his pockets at the cafeteria.

He handed the cashier all the money he had and asked, "What can I buy with that?"

"Many things," said the lady.

He then said he'd like six bubble gums and asked again, "And what else can I buy?"

"Chocolate, ice cream, whatever you like," she continued.

"Then give me two chocolate bars."

When the bell rang, Spender rushed into the classroom, tripped over his feet and spilled all his candy and bubble gum onto the floor. The teacher watched in amazement, as he didn't believe what was happening. There was a lot of noise in the classroom and as soon as all the students got to their seats, Mr. Raymoney continued.

"Very well! From this year on, we'll be learning basic mathematical operations. That is, adding, subtracting, multiplying and dividing. First off, we'll start with adding and subtracting. Later on, we'll get to the other ones. I want you to pay attention to this," he said, writing on the board a problem and the operation.

"Spender had four pieces of bubble gum in his pocket. He went to the cafeteria and bought another 6 pieces. How many pieces of bubble gum did he end up with?"

The class remained quiet and Spender took a chance. "I ended up with 10 bubble gums," he said laughing.

"Very good," the teacher said. "Let's move on to another question."

"Spender had 10 coins when he came to the cafeteria. He used 10 coins to buy bubble gum. How many coins remained with him?"

This time Spender didn't even open his mouth, but Money Boy answered, "He had none left."

"Very good!"

Then Mr. Raymoney walked to the other side of the board and wrote, "Money Boy had no gum. He went to the cafeteria and bought one piece. How many pieces of gum did he end up with?"

"Piece of cake," said Spender with a smile on his face. "He ended up with one single bubble gum."

"Well done. Now let's see another example."

"Money Boy had two coins when he arrived at school today. He used one coin to buy a bubble gum. How many coins did he have left?"

That question Spender didn't even bother answering. Then Money Boy said, "I had one coin left."

"Good job!" the teacher said, leaving the board and returning to his desk. "These are some examples of how we can use math in our daily activities. Now, back to that subject we were discussing before the bell. I want you to think. If we take into account what happened today only, and what's written there on the board, which student is going back home richer today?"

Spender felt his cheeks getting hot. He was so mad his face started getting red. Money Boy was ashamed and didn't say a word.

No one said a word, so the teacher continued.

"In this case, Money Boy is richer or more prosperous than our friend, Spender. That's because Money Boy managed to save a small amount of money, while Spender decided to use all his money buying candy and gum."

Hearing that, Money Boy felt happy, just like he did when his mother praised him, while Spender grew upset and lost his will to say anything.

Then Mr. Raymoney gave the class a homework assignment on the board. "I want you to think about the following question and bring me an answer tomorrow."

To become prosperous, which one is more important: having a great amount of money or knowing how to use money wisely?

The bell rang and it was the end of the school day. Money Boy waved good-bye to the teacher and left in a good mood. He walked out the door and then something awful happened. Spender pushed him hard and Money Boy hit the floor.

"When you get outside, we'll straighten things up, I promise!" Spender yelled.

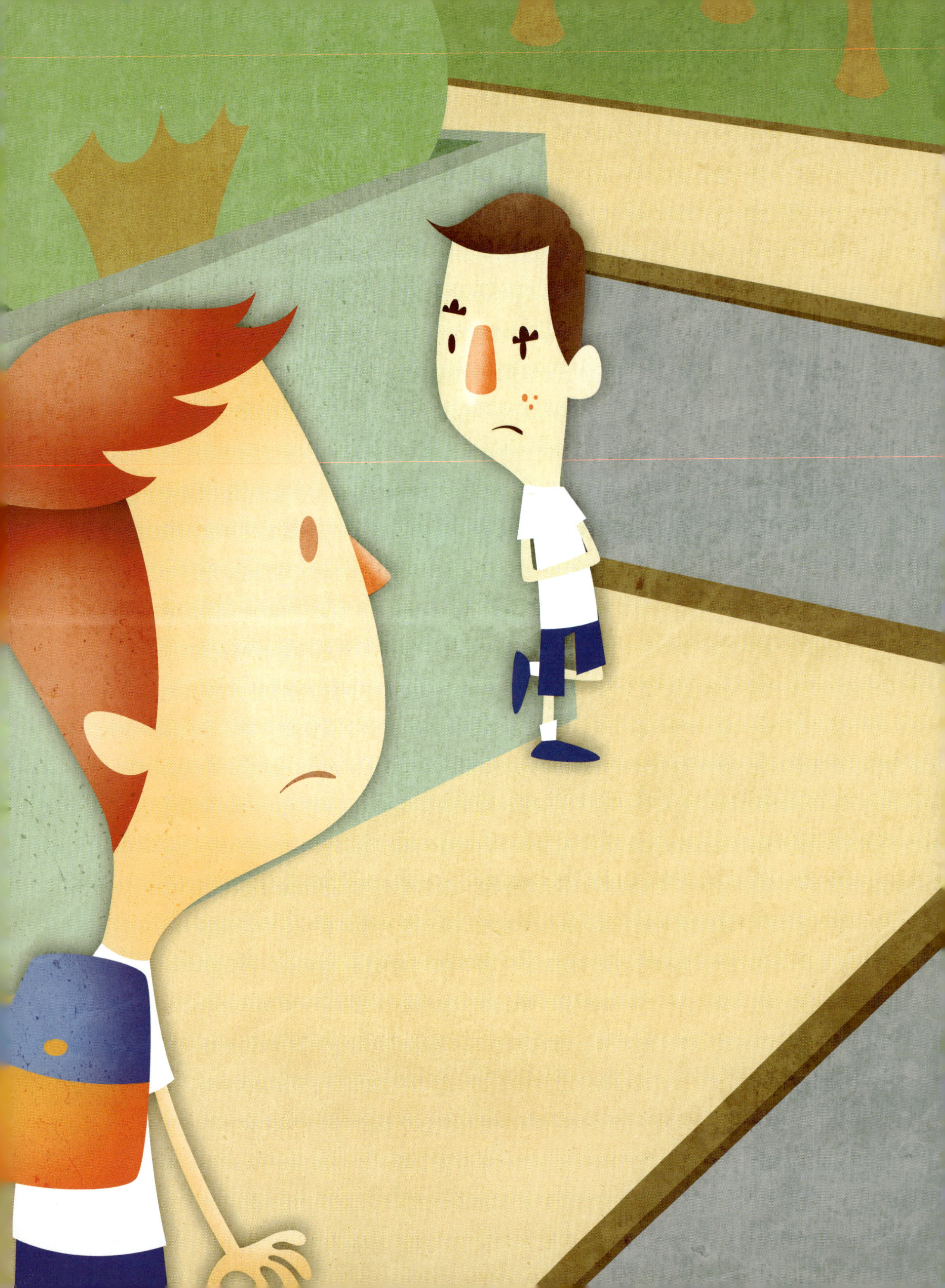

A big mess

Money Boy was wandering around in the schoolyard for a while. Actually, he was afraid of going outside the gate to meet Spender, who was supposed to be waiting for him. *My mother could very well come to pick me up today.*

However, he decided it was about time he had some courage to face his fear. His mother had always told him he should be able to defend himself, because she couldn't physically be by his side all the time to protect him.

Finally, it was the right opportunity to exercise his mother's teachings. Money Boy took a deep breath and marched through the school gate, walking firmly, with his eyes wide open. He spotted Spender right on the first corner, leaning against the wall. The boy wondered if he should cross the street to the other side, but he kept his pace and decided to stand up to the classmate.

As he approached the corner, Spender walked up to Money Boy and gave him a quick shove.

"Now we'll see who's coming home richer!" he shouted, grabbing Money Boy's backpack.

Spender immediately unzipped Money Boy's backpack and grabbed his wallet. Surprised by what he found inside the wallet, he mocked Money Boy even more.

"Well, well, I see you were coming home even richer! With all that money inside your wallet, you are probably thinking you're the school's millionaire."

"Quit it!" cried Money Boy. "Give me back my wallet and leave me alone! That wallet was a gift from my mother."

However, Spender got even more angry and punched Money Boy in the face.

"I don't need your money, because my father is a rich man, not a loser like yours! But I'm keeping your money anyway so you'll learn not to stand in my way," Spender called out, running down the street.

Money Boy felt desperate and hurt over what Spender had just said. His father was a poor man, but he was a hard worker, like his mother used to say. He also was an honest man that had never taken anything from anyone. Spender could very well be rich, but he had done a terrible thing.

Aside from the pain of the punch to his face, he had lost all his money and was worried what his mother would say when he arrived home, hurt and without his wallet.

After a couple of minutes, he managed to stand up and walk home. Maybe he could figure out something to solve this big mess.

Money Boy - Goes to school

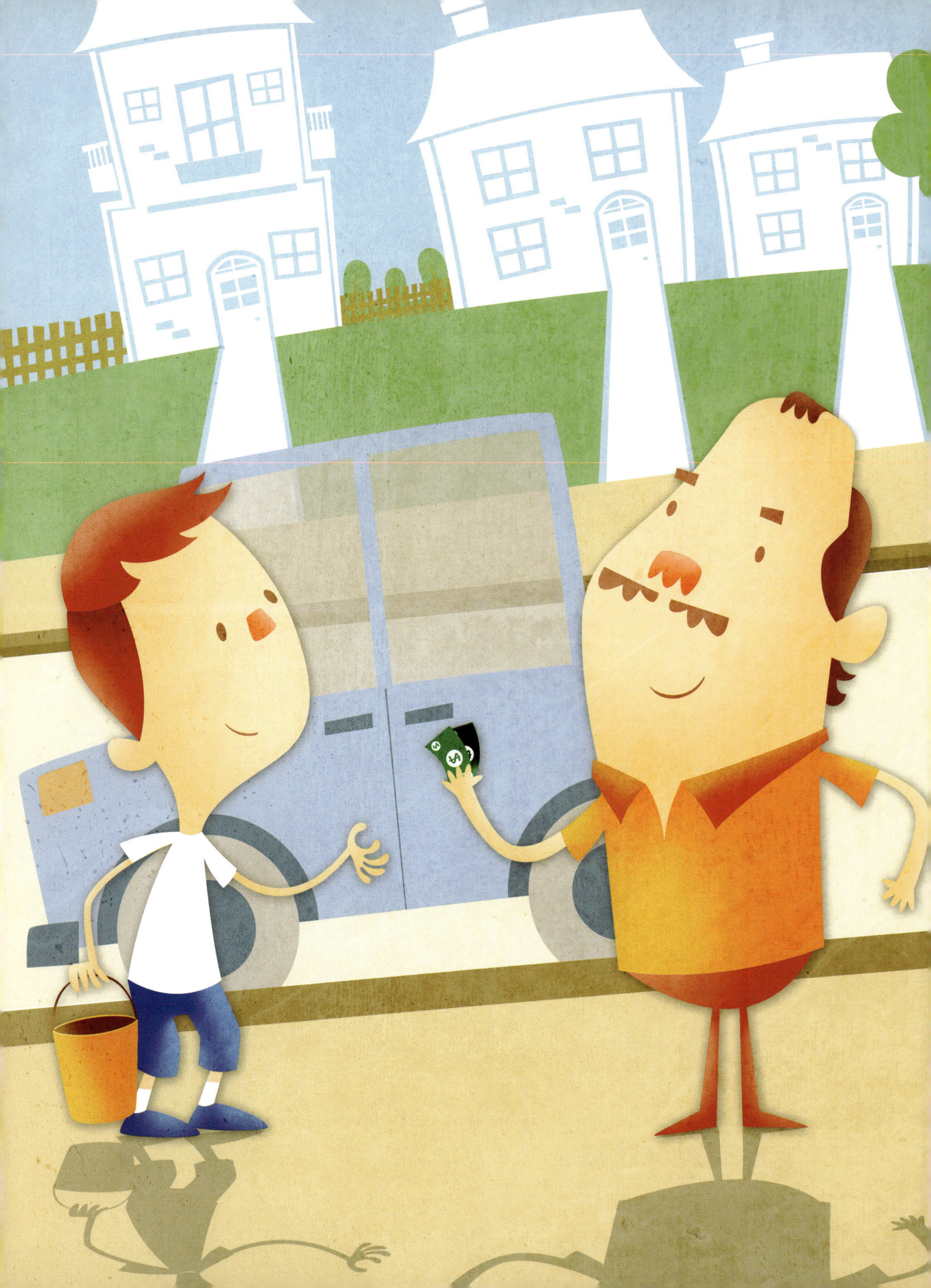

The lie

On his way back home, Money Boy decided to stop over at the gas station to wash his face and drink some water.

When he arrived there, he overheard a conversation from a man who washed the cars.

"We can't do this anymore! We've got to find someone to help us out with the cars. We can't do everything by ourselves anymore."

When he heard that, Money Boy was already thinking of a solution.

After cleaning up, he felt confident again and walked up to the manager.

"Sir, I heard you need someone to help wash the cars here. I may be the one you're looking for."

"You?" said the manager with soap all over his hands. "You're nothing but a kid. You're too young to work! Besides, what about school? I need someone to help us in the morning. Aren't you coming back from school now?"

"No," stuttered the boy. It was the first time he had lied in his life. "I'm on my way to school. But tomorrow morning I can be here from 7:00 to around 11:00," the boy said, trying to fake a clever voice.

"If that's the case, just show up tomorrow at that time and we can try you out. I'll be paying you five dollars a day, plus customer tips."

The boy wanted to ask what a tip was but he thought the manager would get upset with the question and forgot about it.

"Fine with me," the boy nodded. "Don't you want me to stick around for a while and see if I can do the job?"

"I'd like to, but there's a huge line of cars to be washed and you've got to go to school."

"No problem. I'll stick around for just a few minutes and then I'll leave for school."

Money Boy started scrubbing a car. He would stick to the lower parts because he was too short to reach the higher ones. Soon he and the manager cleaned, rinsed, and dried the car.

When they were done, the car owner paid for the service and waved to Money Boy to come over.

"Come here, boy. Come get your tip."

The boy went up to him and got excited when the man handed him a couple of bills.

"That sure was a lucky start, boy!" said the manager. "Not everyone is as generous as that customer. If you remain lucky, you'll keep getting a few dollars like that."

Money Boy, confused with all this new stuff, soon realized that "tip" meant money. He wanted to help wash another car. Maybe someone else would tip him like that.

He couldn't stay too long though, as his mother would get worried. After washing a second car, the customer gave him a bunch of coins and the boy was overjoyed. The boy said good-bye to the manager and told him he would be back the next day.

Money Boy had found a way to get back the bills Spender had taken from him. Only the job at the station would have to remain a secret, because his parents would never let him skip school.

On the way back, he realized that was the first secret he had ever had. The kind of secret you don't tell a soul. He rushed back home, because he didn't want his mother to suspect anything. In fact, Mrs. Foresight didn't even notice that her son came home breathless and with a swollen mouth. When he arrived, she was leaving to go to her customer's house.

"Your lunch is on the table. Eat it up. Then get some rest and do your homework. I won't be long."

Money Boy was relieved that he wouldn't have to explain anything. He did almost everything she told him to do. He ate his lunch, rested on the bed, but didn't do his homework.

He began to think about the question his teacher had asked in the classroom.

To become prosperous, which one is more important: having a great amount of money or knowing how to use money wisely?

Up to that day, the boy believed it was more important to use money wisely. But after the injustice he had gone through, he started to think it might be more important to be wealthy, just like Spender's father, so that no one would ever call his father a loser.

The thought made him sad again and he made up his mind that he would not go to school anymore. He would use his time to work, earn money, and become rich.

When Mrs. Foresight came home and asked about the homework, Money Boy told her he didn't have any actually, he just had to think about some questions.

Because she was very tired and trusted her son, Mrs. Foresight didn't pay much attention to his answer. She just told him to take a shower, eat dinner, and go to bed, since he would have to be up early the next morning.

So, that is exactly what he did.

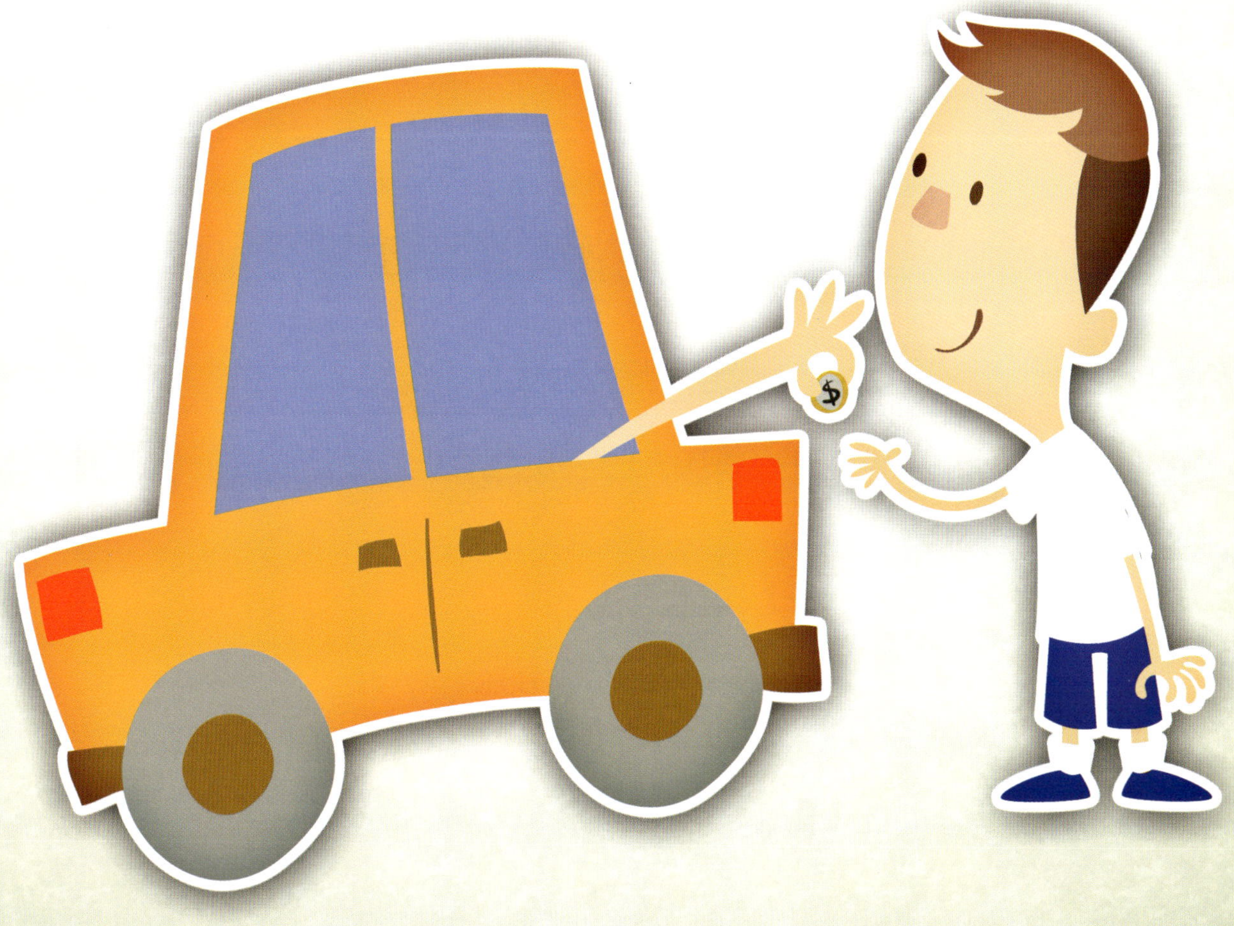

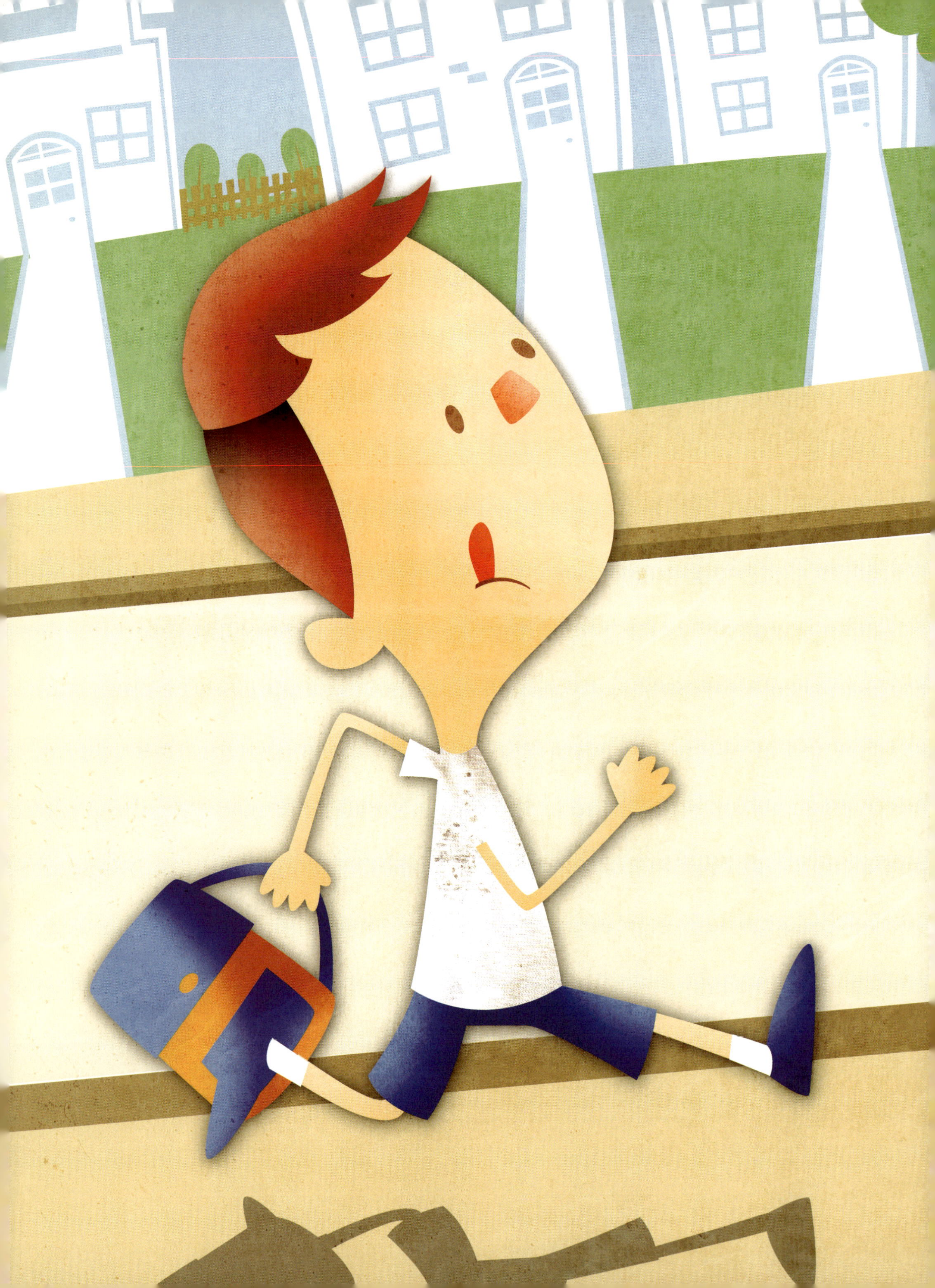

The following day

The following day, Money Boy got ready to go to school as usual, kissed his mother good-bye, and off he went. However, instead of heading to school, he stopped at the gas station to work.

The manager, with whom he had set up everything the day before, felt something was not right when he saw the boy all dressed up in his school uniform.

"Hey kid, didn't you mention you go to school in the afternoon? Why are you in your uniform already?"

Money Boy didn't see that coming and wondered why he hadn't thought of it. He quickly made up an excuse.

"I came in uniform because I'm going to school afterwards," he explained a little awkwardly.

"Is that so, smarty? But you're going to get all dirty washing the cars. How are you going to school afterwards?"

"Ah, that's right. Today I'm going like this, but tomorrow I'll come with some old clothes."

The gas station manager was a little suspicious, but there was already a long line of cars to be washed, and he decided not to give it a second thought.

They worked hard the whole morning. When Money Boy saw some kids walking from school on the other side of the street, he knew it was time to leave.

"I better be going or I'll be late," he said, trying to clean off his uniform.

"Ok, then. Here's your payment," the manager said, giving the boy a five-dollar bill.

Money Boy rushed home, hoping not to be too late. At home, he pretended as though nothing was unusual. Mrs. Foresight found it strange that his uniform was so dirty.

"Were you rolling in the dirt, son? What happened to your uniform?" she said, examining the uniform that had turned from white to brown.

"Today we had gym class, mom," he said, slipping away to his room.

"Ok then. So take a quick shower because lunch is ready."

The boy did as he was told. After showering, he ate a full plate of food and then had another. Washing cars had increased his appetite.

"Why are you so hungry, son?" Mrs. Foresight asked, always a keen observer. "That gym class must have been a tough one, right?"

"Sure was, mom," Money Boy said, hiding his face behind a glass of juice.

"The teacher told us to run around the court several times," he said, feeling bad for telling yet another lie.

"Right then," she said. "How about homework? Do you have any?"

"Not really, just some math problems. I'll get them done quickly."

The boy stood up from the table and escaped to his room, hoping to avoid his mother's questions. Otherwise, he'd have to come up with another lie.

One hour later, Mrs. Foresight came to his room to see how things were going. She was surprised when she saw her son asleep, gripping his notebooks.

She carried him to bed and picked up the pencil and the notebooks. She did see he had solved some addition problems.

Mrs. Foresight concluded they were her son's homework, not knowing he was actually computing the income of his first day's work.

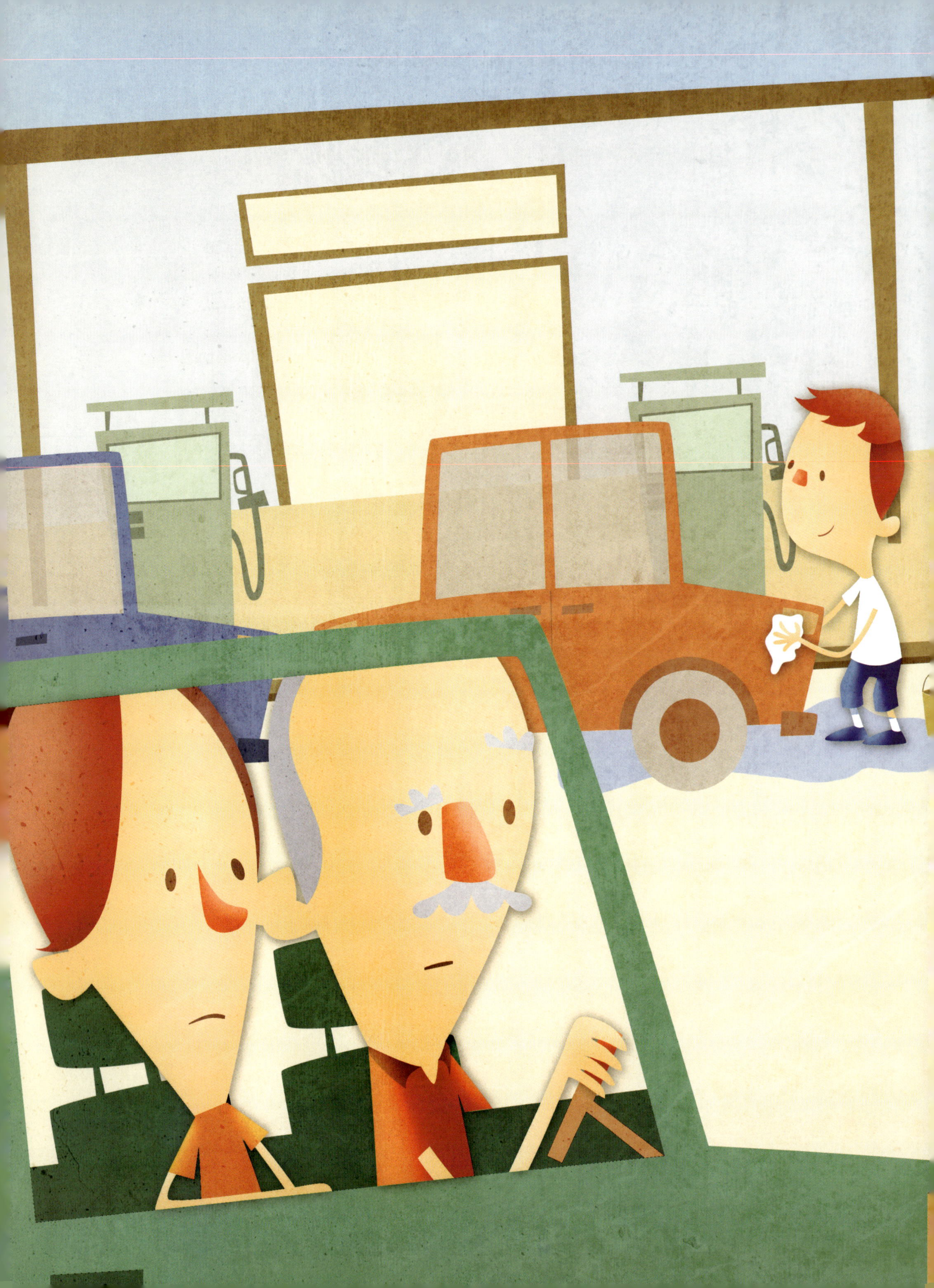

Lies don't travel far

Mrs. Foresight had always taught her son that lying is wrong and can be dangerous. Besides, she used to say lies don't travel far without being caught. Money Boy wasn't aware of it yet, but on that day his lies would get him into trouble.

Without notice, Mrs. Foresight decided to pick her son up at school. She was stunned to see all the kids were gone and her son was nowhere in sight. The instructors began walking out to their cars and Mrs. Foresight ran into the math teacher.

"Are there any students left inside the school?"

"From the morning classes, I believe everybody is gone," Mr. Raymoney said. "Who are you looking for?"

"My son, Money B..., I mean, Ray."

"Oh then, you're Money Boy's mother?"

"Yes sir, I'm very worried. I came here early and didn't see him come out. Is there something wrong?"

The teacher noticed that something weird was going on. He asked Mrs. Foresight to follow him to the teacher's room and offered her a glass of water.

"You must calm down and soon we'll find out what happened," Mr. Raymoney said. "I have to tell you something. It's been three days that your son hasn't shown up at school."

"How can that be possible?" said the mother, turning white as a sheet of paper.

"That's what I'm telling you, Mrs…"

"Foresight. My name is Foresight. And, no, he's not skipping school. Every day he leaves home for school. There must be a mistake!" she said, sounding desperate.

"Stay calm, Mrs. Foresight. I'll take you home. I want to know what's happening to your son, too. He's a smart boy and he must have had a very good reason for not showing up these past few days. Wait here and I'll get my car."

Mrs. Foresight got into the teacher's car and both of them kept talking along the way, trying to figure out what was going on. Mr. Raymoney asked her whether anything different had happened recently. Money Boy's mother was so upset she couldn't recall a thing.

She said that everything seemed normal, that her son would come home at the usual time, and that she couldn't imagine why he had lied to her.

"I'm sure he'll be safe and sound by the time we arrive at your house, just like the other days. Then we'll both talk to him," the teacher said.

As they turned the corner, Mrs. Foresight spotted her son drying a car that had just been washed.

"Look! It's him! I'm so relieved!"

Mrs. Foresight was about to call him over, but Mr. Raymoney stopped her.

"No. Don't call him. We already know he's fine. Now we must figure out exactly what he has been up to. I'll pull over and we'll stay here and watch."

"He's going to pay a huge price for doing that!" said Mrs. Foresight in tears. "So many sacrifices I've made for him and now he's become a liar!"

"Relax, Mrs. Foresight. Don't rush into things. He might have a good explanation for acting like he did."

While they both talked, the mother and teacher watched Money Boy finish washing the cars, get tipped by the customers, and receive his payment from the gas station manager.

They followed him closely as he entered the bathroom and changed his old clothes for his school uniform, and then watched him rush toward home. The teacher, driving his car, and Mrs. Foresight, in the passenger's seat, kept their distance. When they were close to the house, Mr. Raymoney parked the car and they both waited for Money Boy to go inside the home before leaving the car.

"Well, Mrs. Foresight, I believe you want to talk to him."

"By all means," she replied. "You've helped me a lot and if you would join me in this conversation, I'd be very grateful."

"That's fine, but let's hear what he's got to say first."

And, they entered the house.

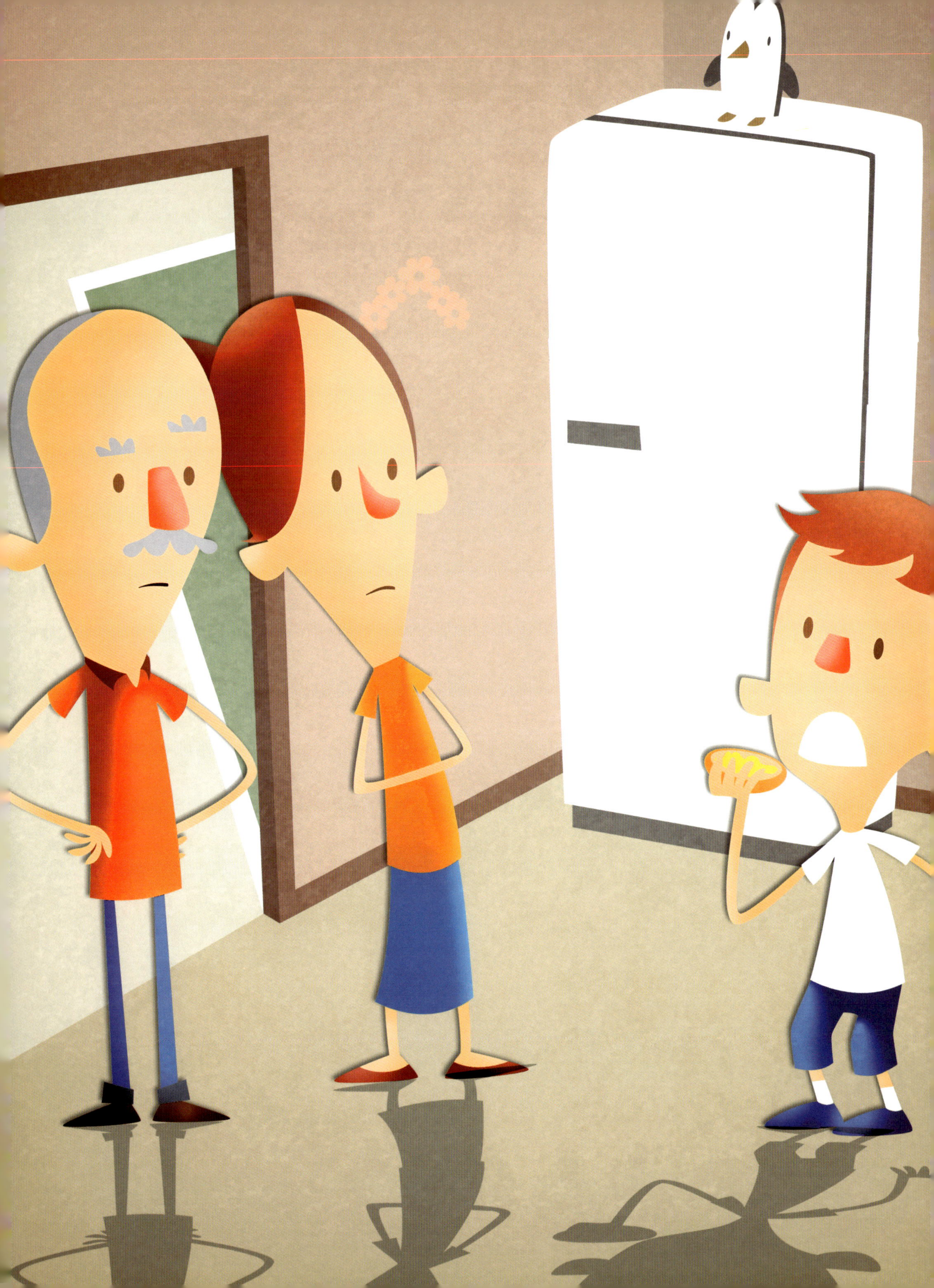

Moment of truth

Money Boy was eating a peanut butter and jelly sandwich when his mother walked into the kitchen. As if her appearance wasn't surprising enough, behind her followed Mr. Raymoney. The boy thought he was going to faint.

Mrs. Foresight stared at him for a very long minute.

"Finish eating your sandwich and take a seat," she said in a serious tone of voice. "I believe we have a lot to talk about."

Money Boy could barely get down the bread with peanut butter stuck in his throat. A sudden rush of water filled his eyes.

He swallowed his bread—and his pride—drank a glass of juice, and sat down at the table with his head down in front of his mother and his teacher.

"So, we're waiting for you, little boy. You may tell us in detail why you've been lying to me," Mrs. Foresight demanded.

Money Boy stuttered to get the words out, "I, I'm sorry, mom. I didn't mean to lie to you."

"And yet you did lie to me. Now it's time to tell the truth. I want the truth. Speak up!"

Money Boy had never seen his mother so impatient. He told her what had happened in the classroom, the fight with Spender, the idea he had in order to regain his lost money, and everything else.

His mother and the teacher let him speak freely without interrupting him. Mrs. Foresight could not stay angry with her son and struggled to hold back her tears.

"How could you hide this from me, son? Why didn't you tell me about the fight? I would have helped you out in another way."

"But mom, I didn't want you to think I was a crybaby. Besides, I found out that earning money is far more important than this studying thing," he said, glancing over at his teacher.

"But son..." the mother was about to continue when Mr. Raymoney interrupted her. "Excuse me, Madam. Since you've invited me in, I'd like to say a few words to your boy."

"Young man," he said, staring at Money Boy. "No doubt you're a very special, very smart boy, but you're mixing things up. Earning money is surely a good thing, but everything has its time. At this point in your life, studying is what matters. That's what is going to make you ready to make your dreams come true later on in life."

"But my mother has always told me that what matters for the future is saving money. The thing is, I lost all the money I saved," the boy said, sobbing. "And school doesn't give anyone any money. I earn a lot more working at the gas station."

Mrs. Foresight was paying close attention to him and couldn't say a word, as she was starting to feel guilty. Fortunately, the teacher was calm enough to reply.

"As a matter of fact, your mother was definitely right when she told you earning money is important and the sooner you realize it, the better. But that's not everything. You have to study first so you can find a job and earn money. You're still a child, regardless of how smart you think you are. And in case you don't know, a child working at your age is a crime," Mr. Raymoney said, emphasizing his words.

When he heard that, the boy realized how serious the situation was.

"Are you saying I've committed a crime?"

"Not exactly. What I'm trying to say is that child labor is forbidden, because it prevents youngsters from being children."

"But I don't want to be a child. I want to be an adult, to have a job and to earn my own money. And, I want to be rich. This way nobody is going to say I'm a loser," the boy said, with tears rolling down his face.

Mrs. Foresight was brokenhearted to see her boy so sad, and the teacher had difficulty hiding his feelings.

Mrs. Foresight then briefly told Mr. Raymoney what she was teaching her son and how he had behaved in the past few years.

"Well," Mr. Raymoney said, looking down at Money Boy. "Just like I am teaching in our classroom, it doesn't matter whether you're rich or poor. What matters is how you use the money you earn. You've shown you already know money deserves respect. You've also shown you are strong-willed and know what you want. Now you have to be patient to make your dreams come true."

"Life is full of challenges, son. This one is just the first one you'll find along the way, but many others are still to come. You've got to be strong and trust the education you receive and not let anything discourage you," Mrs. Foresight added.

The teacher was very impressed with the mother's wise comments.

"I see you've had an outstanding education at home. Now you've got to study and learn new things, to grow up strong," Mr. Raymoney advised the boy.

"But what I really want is to learn more about the magic of money!" Money Boy replied. "My mother told me money has a magic formula that the more you save, the more it grows."

"You're right! Then let's make a deal. Tomorrow you go back to your studies and to your normal life. You promise you'll study hard to learn as much as possible. In return, I'll give you some special lessons about that subject you're so fond of."

Money Boy's eyes were wide open and shining when he heard that.

"But what are you going to teach me?"

"I'll teach you a methodology that will be useful throughout your whole life."

"What's a methodology?"

"Methodology is a technique. Making things simple; it's a way of doing things."

"Way of doing what?"

"In this case, it's a way of making your money grow bigger."

"Wow! That's what I have always wanted to learn. And, what do you call that? Methodo..."

"Meth-od-ol-o-gy," the teacher repeated slowly.

"What do you call that methodology?"

"It's called DSOP. But that's another story, which you'll get to know only if you do your part of the deal."

The boy nodded. Mrs. Foresight finally was convinced her son was back on track. She thanked the teacher for his help and said she would walk the boy herself to school on the following day.

Money Boy gave Mr. Raymoney a big hug and felt as strong as ever and able to face any situation.

With that high spirit, he took his notebooks and, before going to bed, answered the question the teacher had proposed a few days before.

"To become prosperous, which one is more important: having a great amount of money or knowing how to use money wisely?"

Answer: Knowing how to use what you have, learning from people you trust.

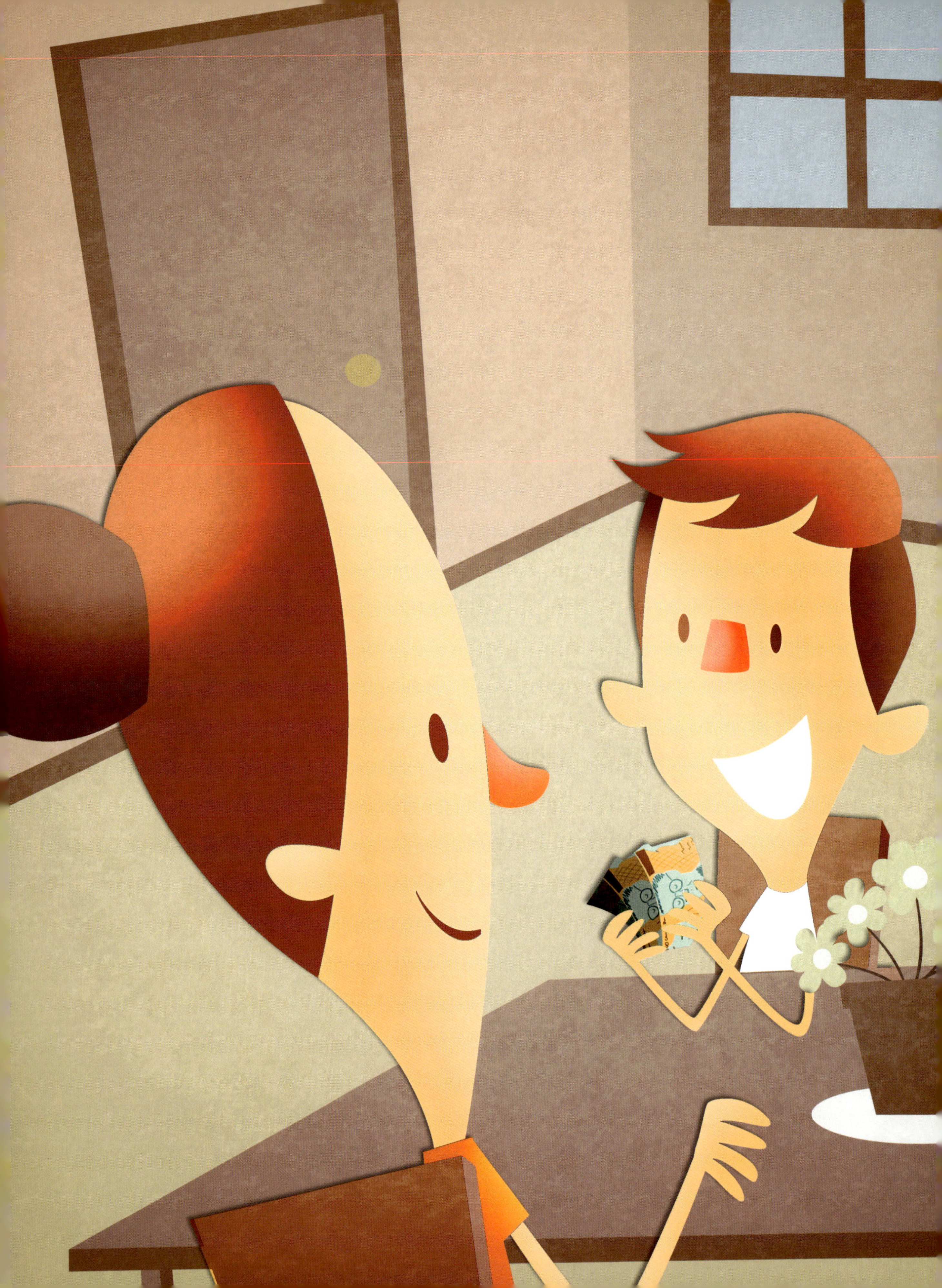

Good news

During breakfast the next day, Mrs. Foresight announced some good news.

"Son, starting today, you will receive a monthly allowance."

"What's that, mom?"

"It's some money you'll receive each month, so you can buy the things you want."

"A salary, you mean?"

"No. A salary is for those who work. You are a child, and children don't work, they just give me work."

"I didn't understand a word."

"Never mind, son. I was just thinking out loud. The thing is that you're going to receive some money each month to use anyway you like. You can focus on studying and forget that crazy idea of working when you are only seven years old. But, one thing is still the same. You've got to take good care of your money," she said, handing the boy seven dollars.

Money Boy was happy and sad at the same time. Mrs. Foresight, who knew him well, soon noticed that.

"What's wrong? You seem sad or am I getting it wrong?" she asked, gently touching his chin to lift his face and look him in the eyes.

"You know, mom. I'm happy with the idea, but I'm sad because I've lost the wallet you gave me. I'll get back the money, that's for sure. Now that I have an allowance, it's going to happen anyway. But the wallet was a birthday present..."

Before her son could finish, Mrs. Foresight started to speak.
"Rest assured, son. You'll get your wallet back with all the money you had in it."

"How's that, mom?"

"That you leave to me. Now go brush your teeth and let's go because we are already late."

Money Boy - Goes to school

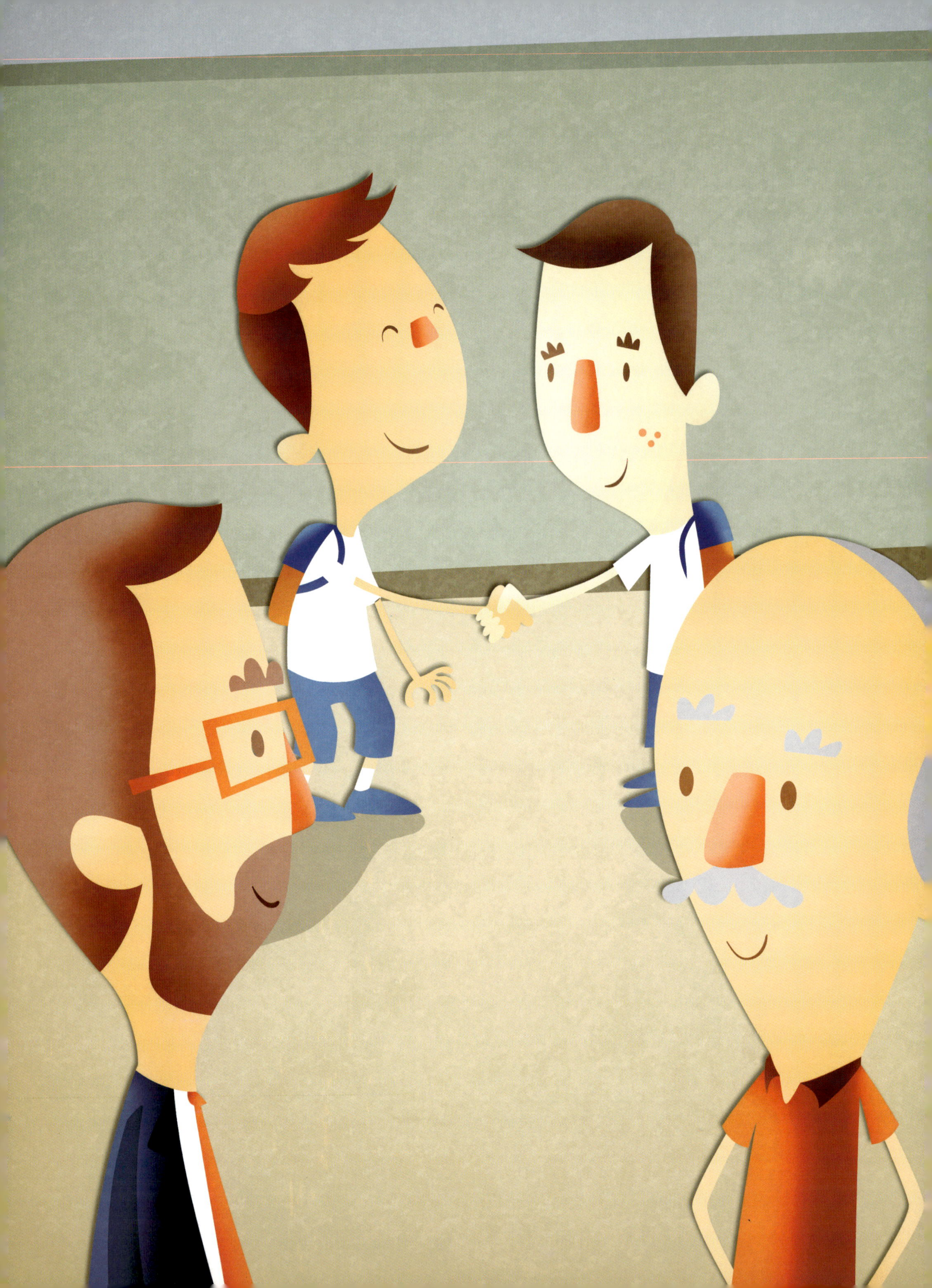

A couple of surprises

When he entered the classroom, his classmates warmly welcomed Money Boy. He turned his attention to Spender's seat, which was empty. The boy was relieved. It'd be great if Spender never showed up at school again, he thought.

Money Boy had just sat down when Spender showed up at the door, followed by a tall and handsome man, dressed in a suit and tie. Both entered the room at the same time as the math teacher.

Money Boy heard the teacher whispering something to the man before he addressed him.

"Ray, could you follow us to my office, please?"

Money Boy was frightened, his mouth was dry, and his legs were shaking. *Who's that man?*

He was imagining the worst possible situation, and the one thought he couldn't get out of his head. *What if that man was a police officer, who would arrest him for staying out of school, or even for working at the gas station? Didn't Mr. Raymoney say, "Child labor is a crime?"*

The boy was so upset by those thoughts that he barely noticed he was already in the teacher's office, facing that man and Spender, who hadn't looked over at him once.

"Well then, Spender. We're all waiting for you," the unknown man said, speaking in the same tone of voice Mrs. Foresight had used when she discovered her son had been lying.

"Here's your wallet," Spender said, handing it to Money Boy without looking at him. The boy took the wallet, feeling relieved that he had gotten it back.

"And what else, Spender?" the man asked. "Let's go, we're waiting. What else have you got to tell us all?"

"I want to apologize for punching you and for taking your money," Spender spoke softly.

"It's okay," Money Boy replied.

"It's not okay, young man. What my son did was very serious and I also offer you my apologies. Rest assured that it will never happen again. Am I right, Spender?" the man asked with a voice that sounded like thunder.

"Yes, father."

"I don't want to take up your time any longer," the man said, shaking hands firmly with the teacher, who then told both students to go back to the classroom.

On his way out Money Boy heard the man talking to the teacher.

"I want to apologize again. I hope my son behaves a little better from now on. I'll do my best to follow him closely. You know, raising a kid without a mother is not easy."

When he heard that, Money Boy felt he was no longer mad at Spender. *He doesn't have a mother,* he realized. Spender passed in front of him with his head hanging down.

Money Boy ran up to his classmate before entering the room and touched his shoulder.

"We can be friends if you want to," he suggested, stretching his arm to shake hands with Spender.

Surprised by the gesture, Spender looked up and shook the boy's hand.

"Deal. No fighting anymore."

"No more fighting," replied Money Boy.

On that day, Mr. Raymoney kept on explaining math with addition and subtraction problems, but he didn't use money as examples.

"Paul had five baseball cards. He then won another three cards from his friend Peter. How many cards did he have in total?"

The kids drew images in their notebooks, added them up, and talked about the results.

"Laura had nine colorful marbles in her collection. She gave her friend Alice three marbles. How many were left?"

Then the kids drew the marbles, completed the subtraction, and said the results out loud.

Mr. Raymoney gave them ten more problems, all of them very similar, and kept repeating that the students should practice more.

Money Boy paid close attention, but he didn't understand why the teacher kept changing the examples.

When the class was about to end, Mr. Raymoney told Money Boy to wait a while longer because he wanted to talk to him.

Money Boy - Goes to school

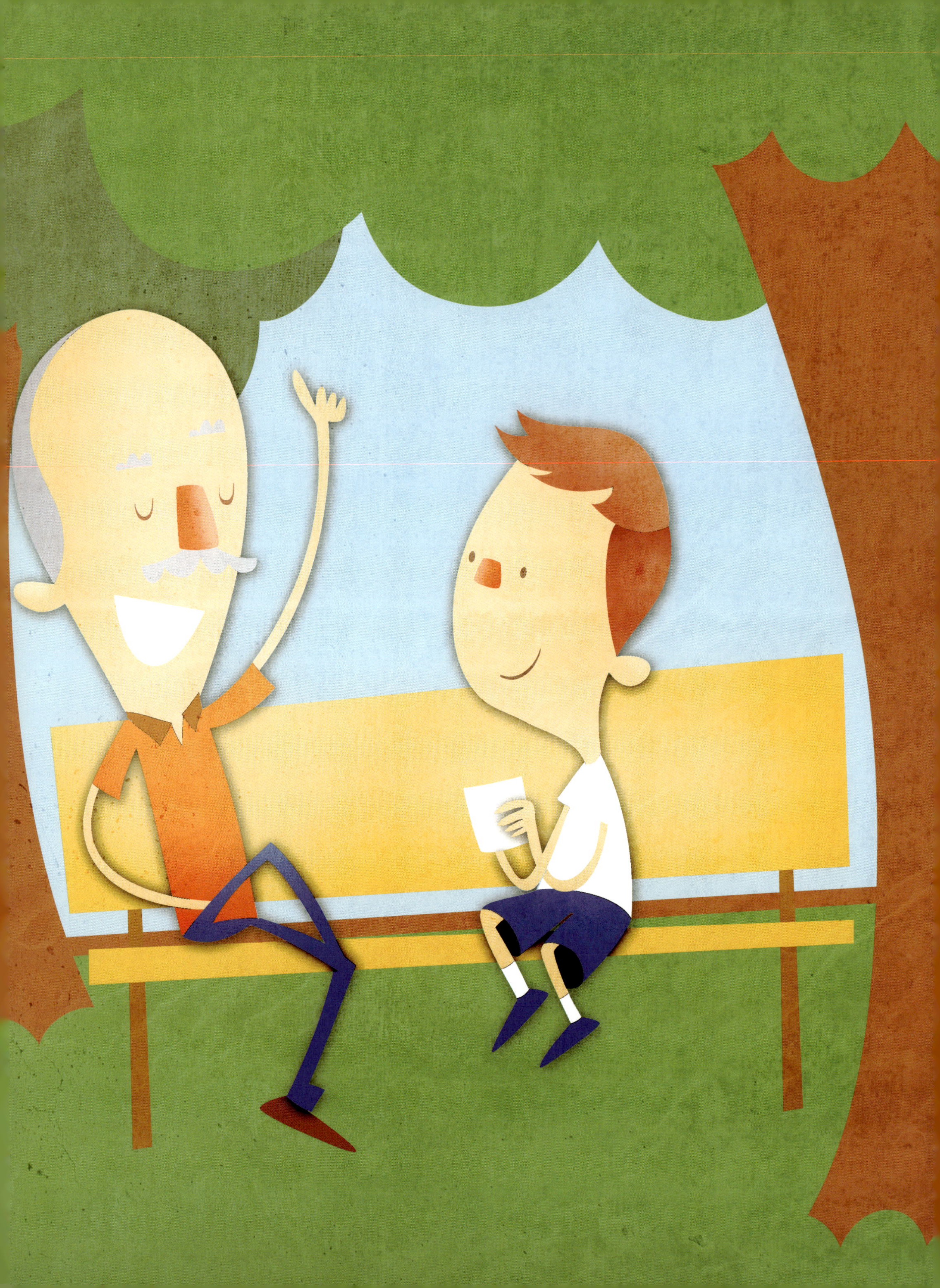

The treasure map

After storing his books in a locker, the teacher asked Money Boy, "So, are you ready to learn the first lesson of DSOP Methodology?"

"Sure I am! I was waiting for this during the whole class."

"Very well, let's get going. I want to talk to you at that park over there, near the school. Nature is always a good inspiration for learning."

After arriving at the park, they took a seat under a huge fig tree and the teacher started to speak.

"Here we are. I'm going to share with you something I have learned and used in my own life, and it has helped me achieve my financial independence," Mr. Raymoney said.

"What do you mean by financial independence?" the boy asked.

"People can be financially independent if they do not need their salary to make a living."

"By salary, you mean?"

"Yes, salary. If people are financially independent, it means that they don't use their salary to pay for monthly expenses. They can, for instance, lose their job and still be able to make a living."

"But how can that be possible? My father keeps saying he fully depends on his salary, and yet he complains it's not enough."

"Precisely! Like your father, most people experience financial difficulties because they don't know how to deal with money."

"You see how I was right? That's why I want to learn what this money thing is all about," the boy said.

"You are absolutely right in thinking like that. Luckily, your mother has taught you the importance of saving some of the money that comes into your hands for future dreams and wishes. Many people spend their whole life without saving a single penny," Mr. Raymoney continued.

Money Boy felt good just thinking about the coins in his piggy banks and, more recently, the bills in his wallet, especially since Spender had given all of it back to him

"I already have some money. It's not much, but do you think I can be independent with it alone?"

"Today what you have is not enough. But if you have the discipline to keep saving, you'll certainly become independent sooner than you think."

"That would be great for sure. What I really want is for my father to be independent. He keeps saying that life is harsh. I got him a piggy bank, because I thought he would make some wishes with it, but I don't think my plan worked out very well. Do you think only children can become independent?"

"Not at all! Of course, the sooner you start saving money, the faster you'll have an amount that's enough to become independent. Even adults can begin building their own independence. Unfortunately, your father never had anyone to teach him that."

"Then I want you to help me build my father's independence," the boy said, as if he had mastered that big word.

"That's a great idea! Let's do this. I'll teach you and you teach him."

Money Boy was overjoyed with that idea. "So, what can I teach him today, for example?"

"What have you learned today?"

"I've learned that it's important to be financially independent, and that means a person doesn't need a salary to make a living."

"Very good!" Mr. Raymoney said. "There is also an important element that we shouldn't forget. Achievement is only possible if one really, really wants it to happen."

"Who wouldn't want to?"

"There are people who want to achieve but are not willing to make the necessary effort. It's like wanting to win a race without ever practicing."

"I get it," the boy said without having actually understood.

"We're done for today. You've learned what it is to be independent and why it is important. Now you need to go home. If it takes too long, your mother is going to be worried."

"But that methodology thing you'd mentioned?" Money Boy insisted.

"The DSOP Methodology is like a path people need to follow to finally arrive at their independence. It's like a treasure map, let's say."

Money Boy just loved the idea of a treasure map and his eyes were shining with curiosity. The teacher noticed it, but before the boy could say another word, Mr. Raymoney ended the conversation.

"We'll talk about that tomorrow. Now go home, get some rest, do your homework, and think about what we have discussed."

Money Boy - Goes to school

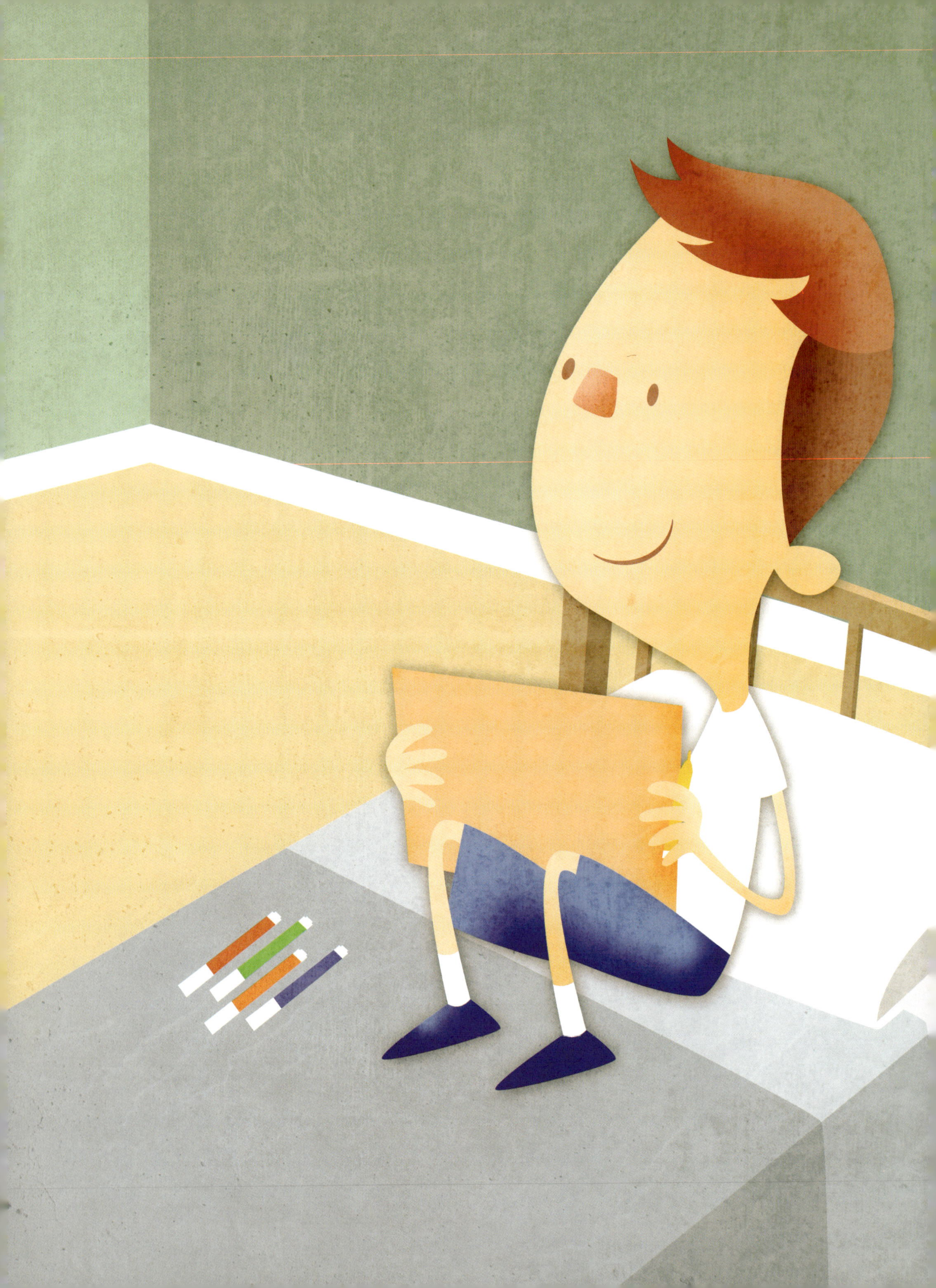

First lessons

When he arrived home, Money Boy found his mother waiting for him at the front door.

"I was about to go after you. What took you so long, may I ask?"

"Today I had my first extra lesson with Mr. Raymoney. Every day, after school, he's going to teach me something about the magic of money."

"Well, I heard him promise that. What's this Mr. Raymoney thing? As far as I know, his name is Raymond," Mrs. Foresight said.

Money Boy told his mother the whole story about the teacher's name and the fact that they had the same name twice.

When he finished his story, his mother looked at him proudly.

"You see son, you've already learned many wonderful things! I hope you won't be skipping classes anymore so that you get the most out of school. I didn't have the opportunity to study much, but I know how important education is in life."

"I know that mom. Trust me, I'll do everything right this time. The teacher also said that if I am to become financially independent, studying is a major step toward that goal. "

"I see! So you think you can be financially independent at this age?"

"Not now, mom. In the future, yes. Mr. Raymoney told me the sooner we start building our financial independence, the better."

"I see."

"That was my first lesson. I won't say anymore now, because I want to tell daddy all about it when he arrives home. Can we talk about it after dinner?"

"I'm fine with that, but I'm not sure your daddy will be willing to talk about this subject."

"I'll handle it, mom. I think I can find a way to start talking. I just need you to back me up."

"All right!" Mrs. Foresight said. "Until then, you already know the drill."

"Yes, mom. Take a shower, get some rest, do my homework."

"That's it. If your homework isn't done by dinner, there will be no talking afterwards."

"Deal!" The boy ran to his room

When evening came, the boy had finished everything his mother had asked of him. He recalled his earlier conversation with Mr. Raymoney and made some notes in his notebook. That way, it would be easier to remember everything he wanted to tell his father. He wrote:

1. What does it mean to be financially independent?

Answer: Not depending on a salary to make a living.

2. What do people need to learn to be financially independent?

Answer: To learn how to save a small amount of their earnings.

3. Can anyone become financially independent, regardless of age?

Answer: Yes, it's just a matter of wanting.

4. How can that be possible?

Answer: By using the DSOP Methodology.

5. What is the DSOP Methodology?

Answer: It's a treasure map that shows how to achieve financial independence.

Money Boy felt very sure of himself when he finished writing. He learned exactly what his teacher had told him. If he were to take a test about it, he would get the highest score. He had all the answers.

The boy ripped the page out of the notebook and stuck it inside his pocket. If he forgot anything when he was speaking to his father, he would have all the notes at hand.

Mr. Unaware finished dinner and was about to leave the table when the boy approached him.

"Daddy, are you very tired today?"

"You bet, son! What's up?"

"I need your help with my homework," the boy said, winking his eye at his mother.

"Your mother is the one that helps you with your homework. Tomorrow she'll help you."

"But the teacher said this assignment should be done with the father."

"Don't these teachers know that we spend the whole day working and now this?"

"The homework is actually about that, daddy, and how people like you who work every day, all month long, and yet, never get to be financially independent."

Hearing that, Mr. Unaware sat himself back at the table and pushed away the empty plate in front of him.

"Ok then, let's go. What are the questions? I'll try to answer some of them."

The boy took the sheet of paper out of his pocket and started questioning his father. Already, Mr. Unaware didn't know how to answer the first question.

As he had written the answers himself, the boy gave the answer to each question.

"Being financially independent is not depending on a salary to make a living?"

The boy's father sat up in the chair, crossed his arms, and started to speak.

"Now this is only true if you're rich, because a poor man depends totally on his salary."

Money Boy then recalled what the teacher had told him that day.

"My teacher said people can be rich even if they don't make a lot of money. And they can be poor even if they make a lot of money."

"Oh, really? May I ask how your teacher thinks that's possible?"

"Learning from the very beginning how to save a small amount of the money you make," the boy responded, after consulting his sheet of paper.

Money Boy's father scratched his chin and thought it over.

"Yes, that's true. If people, even rich people, spend their money to the last penny, they will become poor overnight. Poor people have to save, to live a little better day by day. Take us for example. We managed to buy this house with the money we earned from working."

Money Boy felt very happy to hear his father talk like that. For the first time, he did not complain that life was hard.

"Daddy, Mr. Raymoney is going to teach me a method to achieve that. Buying toys, cars, and houses—everything we want—besides saving some money, of course."

"But how is he going to teach that?"

"He's going to teach me a methodology."

"And what's this methodology all about?"

"It's a way of doing things. My teacher told me that methodology is like a treasure map, which helps people achieve their dreams and conquer their financial independence."

"Well then, you tell your teacher I want to follow up on this closely. I don't want a stranger teaching my son about a treasure map without me knowing exactly what it is all about."

He glanced over to his wife, "Keep an eye on this kid. I don't want anyone taking him off the right path."

"Be calm, honey," Mrs. Foresight said, who had been silent up to that point. "I know the teacher, and he's a serious man who is teaching our son many good things."

"Ok then. I'm going to bed now, but tomorrow I want to hear more about this subject.

Money Boy was happy with the results. He thought his father had really become interested in the methodology, because he wanted to talk about it again the next day.

The boy went to bed anxious to learn new things and teach them to his dad.

DIAGNOSE

DREAM

BUDGET

SAVE

Diagnose

The next day after school Money Boy waited for his teacher at the same spot as the day before. As soon as Mr. Raymoney arrived and took a seat, the boy told him about his recent conversation with his father. He assured the teacher that his father was very interested in learning more, so they didn't have any time to lose.

"Okay," Mr. Raymoney said, opening his briefcase and taking out a notebook. "Today I'm going to introduce you to the DSOP Methodology."

Immediately, the boy held a firm grip on his notebook to begin writing down everything that the teacher had to say. He would have to provide the information to his father when he arrived home.

The acronym DSOP consists of four initial letters of the words in Portuguese, which makes up the methodology.

D is for Diagnosticar (Diagnose)

S is for Sonhar (Dream)

O is for Orçar (Budget)

P is for Poupar (Save)

"When someone learns how to put these four magical words into practice in their financial life, everything gets better. Your money goes a lot further, you can make your dreams come true, and you start to build your financial independence," Mr. Raymoney explained.

Money Boy's eyes were open wide, holding onto every word the teacher said.

"The first step is to Diagnose, that is, mapping your financial life and taking notes of everything you earn and spend. By doing so, you'll be able to do a better job of tracking the path your money is making," the teacher said.

"Can I do that, even if I get only a monthly allowance?"

"Can and should," the teacher answered. "How much is your allowance?"

"I get $7 a week, so it's $28 a month."

"Well then. You know exactly how much your income is. However, many people don't know that, because they have no control over it."

"Do you think my father knows his?"

"You should ask him that yourself. It's very important that he is aware of how much he earns and, especially, how much he spends on everything he buys. Only then will he be able to control his money."

"And how can he do that?"

"First, take notes of his daily expenses in this 30-Day Expense Notebook. You, too, should do the same with your expenses," instructed the teacher, taking three small notebooks from his briefcase.

"Can I have one of these?"

"Sure! I also brought one for your father and another one for your mother, because it's important for the whole family to be a part of this. You can begin registering your expenses at once, but you have to divide each expense according to its type. For example: candy, ice cream, and stickers. You fill out one sheet for each type of expense and at the end of the month, you'll know exactly how much you've spent on each one."

Money Boy's head was full of questions. "And after that, what should I do?"

"You have to check whether you're spending more than you should on anything in particular and decide what isn't necessary. After that, you have to find a way to cut some necessary expenses."

"Let's say you buy a lot of candy, for example. You can eliminate that. Besides, sugar isn't good for your health anyway. But, of course, you shouldn't skip your lunch. You can save some money by bringing fruit and a sandwich from home, instead of buying them at the cafeteria. You'll probably be eating healthier, too. In the end, you'll be able to save more money for your dreams."

"To become independent?" the boy asked?

"Yes, to become independent or to achieve a dream you might have."

"I've been doing that, because my mother taught me as a little boy to save some coins."

"That's excellent! With that attitude, and staying disciplined, you'll be able to achieve everything you want."

"What about my father? Do you think he will be able to become independent?"

"First of all, that depends on the diagnostics. We need to learn which path his money has been following, so we can find a way to give that money a smarter destination."

"Will you help me with that?"

"I will. It will also be a great exercise for what I'm teaching you. Let's do this.

Today you're going to take home the Expense Notebooks: One for you, one for your mother, and one for your father. Start filling them up, and tomorrow we'll talk more."

Before saying good-bye, he asked Money Boy, "So, what have you learned today?"

"I've learned that DSOP Methodology's magical words are the way to achieve financial independence," the boy responded. "They are diagnosing, dreaming, budgeting, and saving."

Mr. Raymoney continued to quiz the boy with a series of questions on everything he had taught him.

"And how can you diagnose or map your financial life?"

"Writing down everything I buy in the Expense Notebook."

"So you can do what afterwards?"

"Cut out the unnecessary expenses."

"Only that?"

"No. I also need to reduce the necessary ones."

"How?"

"Look for new alternatives."

"Very good!" cheered the teacher. "You are a quick learner. Tomorrow we'll move on."

Money Boy - Goes to school

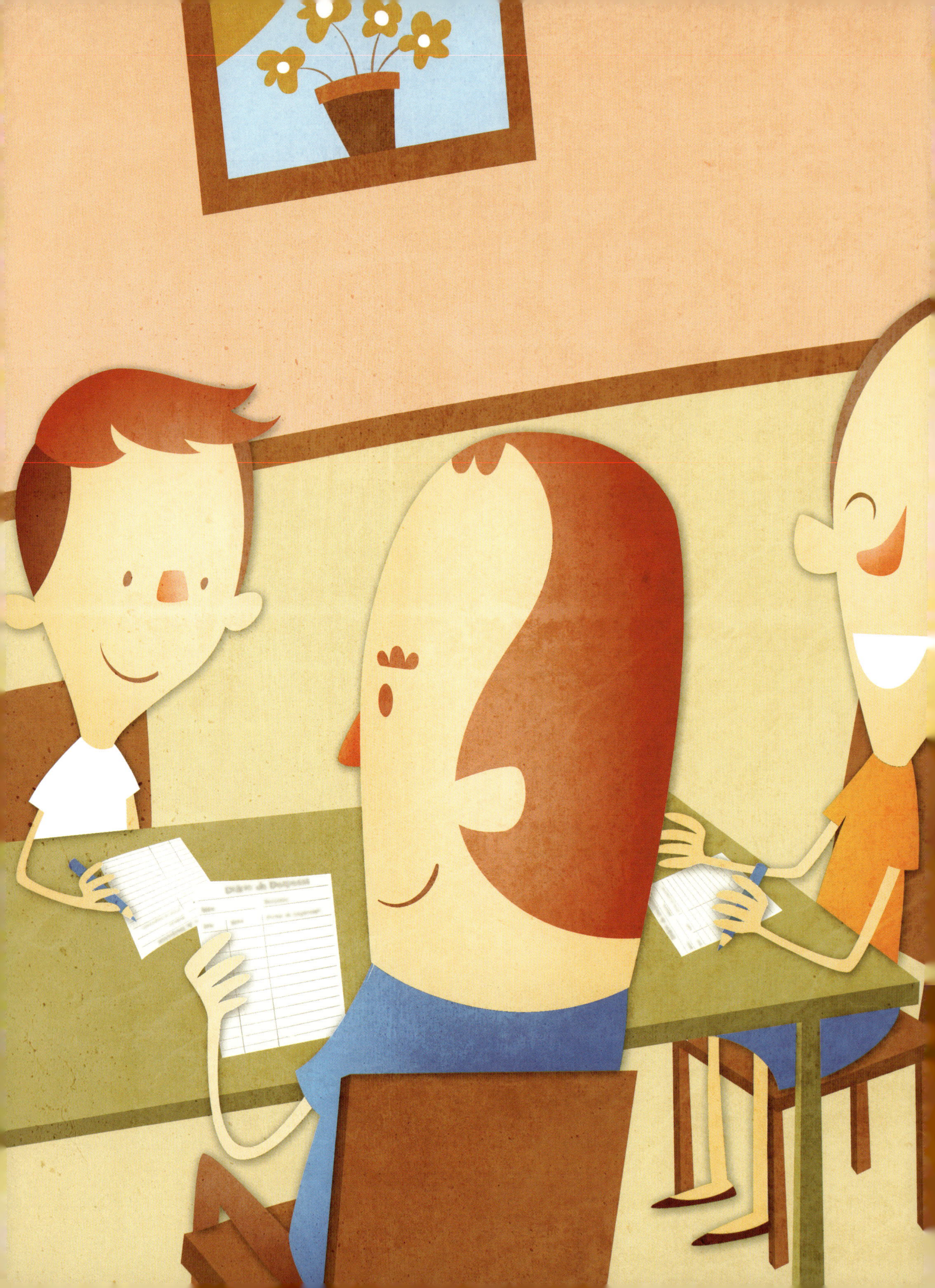

Family that thinks together

That night, Money Boy repeated the exercise he had done the day before. After finishing all his daily duties, including his homework, he thought about what Mr. Raymoney had told him.

Then he sat down and made a brief summary, writing down questions and answers. That way it would be easier for him to grasp what he had learned. He wrote:

1. What does DSOP stand for?

Answer: D for Diagnose, S for Dream, O for Budget, and P for Save.

2. What is diagnosing in DSOP Methodology?

Answer: It is tracking down your money's path.

3. Why is it so important to diagnose?

Answer: Because if you know how much your income is and how much you spend, saving becomes easier.

After dinner, Money Boy didn't even have to mention the subject. As soon as he had finished eating, Mr. Unaware, instead of going to the veranda, remained seated. He looked at his son and started to ask him some questions.

"Son, what else did your teacher tell you about that subject?"

Money Boy realized his father was truly interested, and then he made an effort to repeat every word the teacher had said, pronouncing the words syllable by syllable, because he wanted to show his father he was a smart boy.

His effort was not in vain. As he was explaining, the father paid more attention and sometimes would interrupt the son to ask a question.

"But how can I track down my money's path if after I earn my salary, it's gone before I get home? I stop by the bank to pay the bills and there's nothing left in the end."

"According to the teacher, you should write down everything in the Expense Notebook, placing each expense on a different page."

"Really? That's not a bad idea. This way I'll be able to know exactly where the money went," the father said.

"And you'll be able to reduce expenses as well," the boy added.

"Reduce what, son? We don't spend money on anything but the basics."

"The teacher says that small expenses are the ones responsible for making money disappear. Vanish away, like you said."

Mr. Unaware stared at his son as though he was the teacher.

"Maybe you're right, you know! A cup of coffee here, a magazine there, a tip sometime... If we sum up everything... You know what? Let's fill up that Expense Notebook, because I want to follow closely what my money has been up to," the father said.

The boy and his father spent a whole hour filling in the notebook with the expenses of the day: father helping the boy, boy helping the father.

Mrs. Foresight watched from afar and kept silent the entire time.
She didn't want to spoil the contact between father and son that she had never seen before.

Wise as she was, Mrs. Foresight soon felt encouraged to make a list of her expenses. She wanted to trace the path of the money she made by selling jewelry and cosmetics. Who knows, maybe one day she would have her financial independence as well.

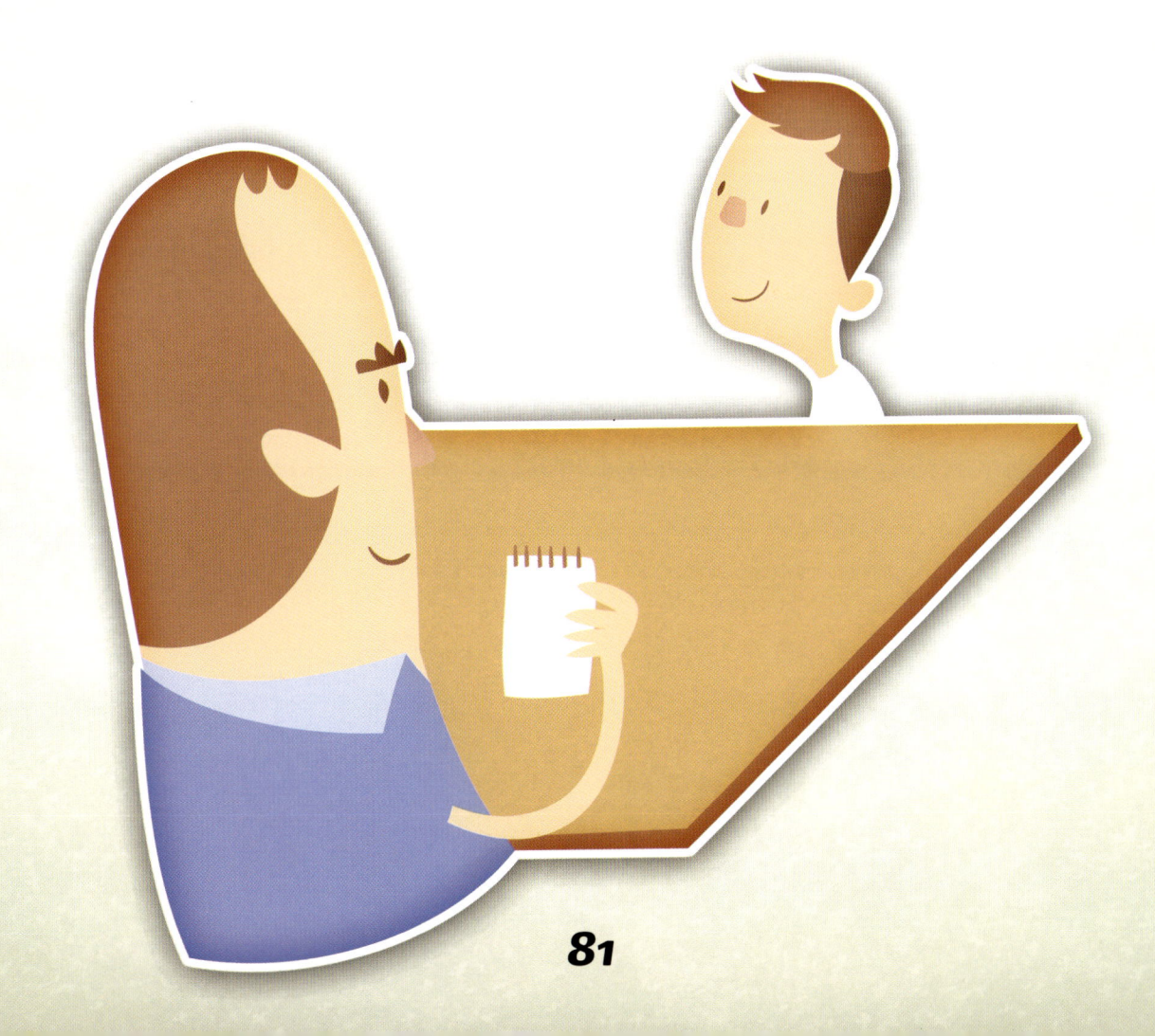

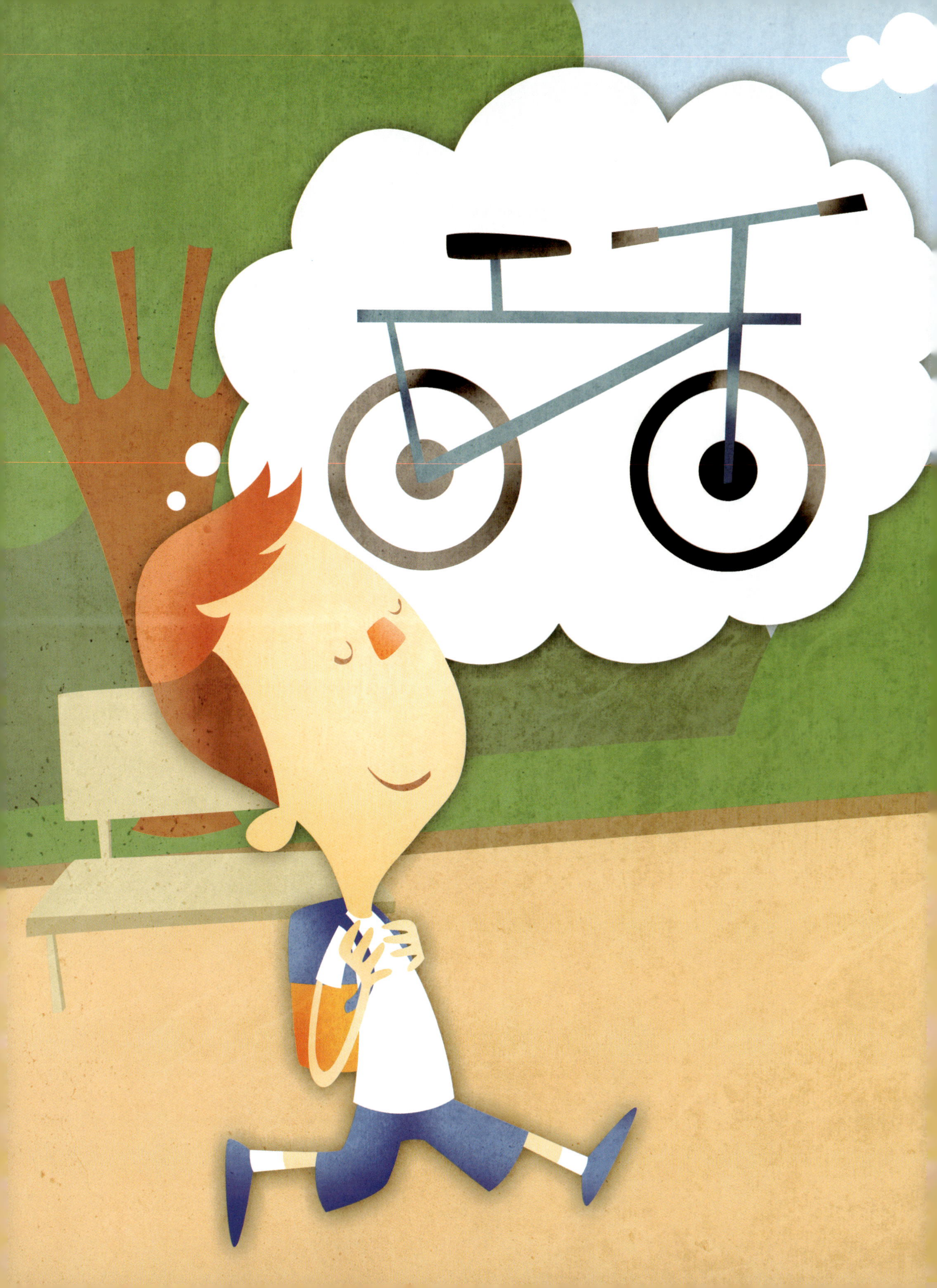

Dreaming

The following day, at the same spot, Money Boy and the teacher met again. Upon arriving, the teacher saw the boy had the notes in his hand.

"So then? I see you've done your homework, right?"

"Yes I did and so did my dad. Take a look at his notes," handing the teacher the Expense Notebook.

"Very good! You've written down everything you spent yesterday, that's great. But now, you have to keep taking daily notes for the next 30 days. Only then will you have a full picture of your money path," Mr. Raymoney said.

The boy looked a little disappointed, "You mean I won't have anything to teach my father today?"

"No, just the opposite. Like I said, you have to stick to your diagnosis throughout the month and repeat it every year, because income and expenses are always changing. At the same time, you must address the second step of our methodology."

"Dreams?" the boy asked.

"That's it! You've learned part of this step from your mother, when she encouraged you to save a small amount of your coins in order to buy things later. Your mother, in fact, has taught you a way to make your dreams come true. Now you'll be able to achieve even greater dreams for yourself and for your parents. For example, do you know what your biggest dream is?"

The boy didn't need to think very hard to answer. "My biggest dream is to have a bike. But I know I would have to save lots of coins to buy one, because it's very expensive."

"That's true, a bike is not a cheap dream. If you do everything right, you'll be able to have your own bike within a year. You just cannot rush into things," Mr. Raymoney advised.

"How can I be sure I'll be able to buy a bike one year from now?"

"What will guarantee that is your ability to save money to make your dream come true. The more you save, the sooner it will happen."

"What if I'm able to save just a little each month?"

"It would take you a longer time, but you could still get what you wanted. Therefore, you better have a short-term dream, a medium-term dream, and a long-term dream," the teacher suggested.

"I don't think I'm getting it," the boy replied, looking confused.

Mr. Raymoney went on to explain. "For a child, a short-term dream would be one that could be achieved within one month. It would take six months for a medium-term and one year for a long-term dream. Your bike dream is a long-term dream."

"Okay, now I think I got it. My wish is to own a bike one year from now, and a skateboard within six months, and a soccer ball for next month."

"Precisely! That's why the first page of your Expense Notebook is reserved for registering your short-, medium-, and long-term dreams. It's important that you save money for the three of them simultaneously. So, it would be good to always have three different piggy banks."

"But I don't know if my father also has a dream. I gave him some coins but he couldn't even think of a dream he wanted to come true when his piggy was full.

"You see, like many people, your father has forgotten how to dream, because he thinks he won't have money to make that dream happen. And that's exactly where the mistake is. When we have a dream, we become more motivated to make the necessary effort to make it happen."

"Then you think my father will make his dreams come true?"

"If he follows the methodology steps, yes I do. Everything's a matter of changing habits, reviewing old customs, and respecting money. But I think it's enough for today, don't you?"

"Okay," the boy agreed, closing his notebook. What would be my daddy's dream?

"Ask him that. Afterwards, ask him to make his dream a priority. Then, every month, before paying the bills, your father must save an amount of his earnings to make his dream happen."

"But my father keeps saying there's nothing left out of his money. How could he possibly spare some money for his dream?"

"The dream must be his top priority. That's why he needs to save money for the dream before anything else. He can't wait for some extra money to achieve what he wants. His dream has to be the first priority."

"But... What if there's no money left for the bills?"

"If he notices there is not enough money for the bills, he'll have to go back to diagnose and try to find out a way to reduce them even more, and that includes basic bills like water, electricity, gas, telephone, and food."

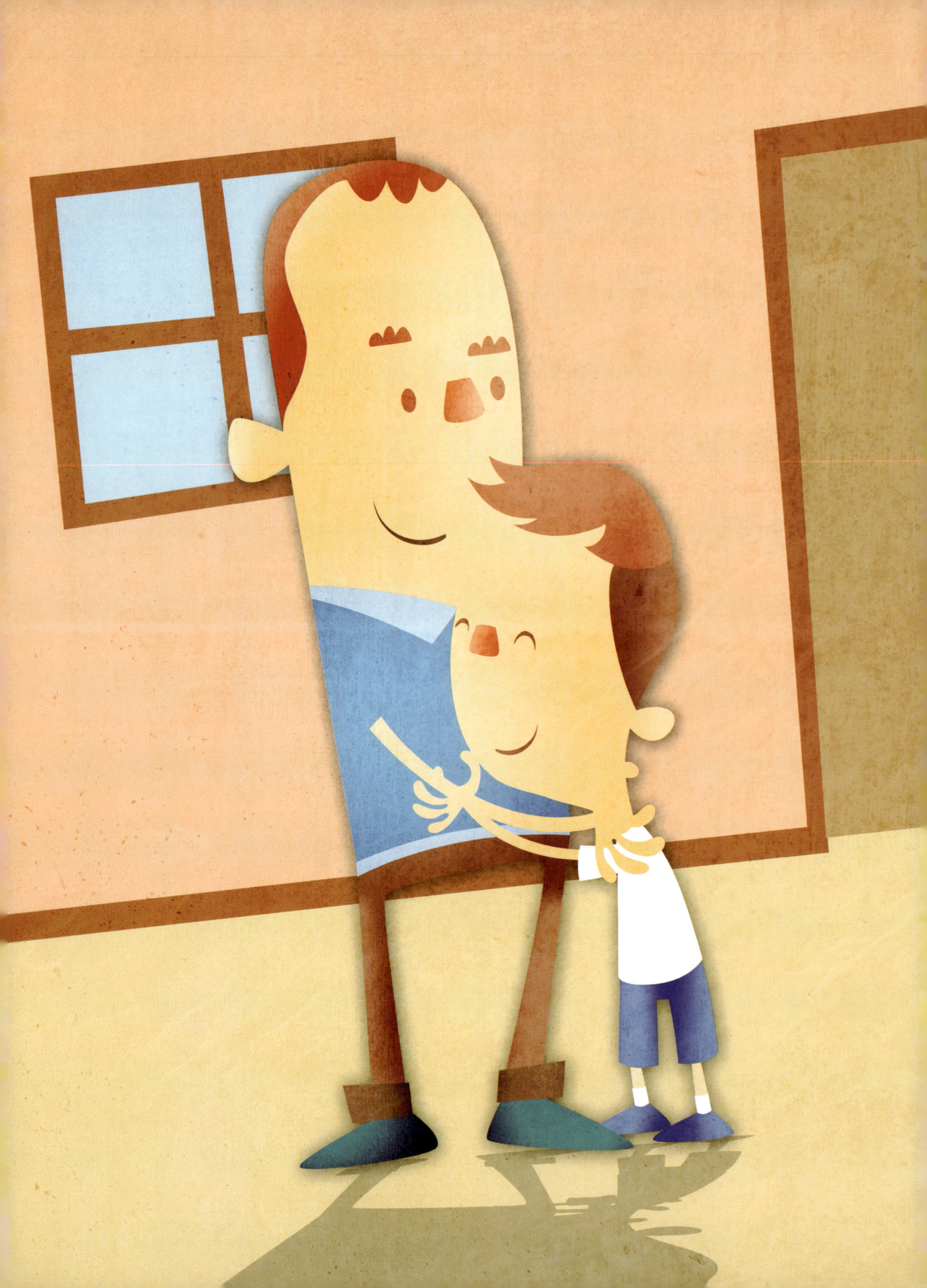

Son's dreams and father's dreams

This time Money Boy didn't wait to come home to come up with his summary. At the park, he took a sheet of paper and recalled the most important sections of the chat he just had with the teacher.

1. Taking notes of all the expenses, every single day, to build a full picture of the money path.

2. Think of three dreams you want to make happen.

3. Set a short-, a medium-, and a long-term dream.

4. Make the dream a priority, before any expense.

5. Analyze each expense and reduce it down in order for the dreams to be in the first place.

That evening, when Mr. Unaware sat at the table to talk with his son, the boy asked,

"Daddy, what's your dream?"

"Son, I don't have many dreams in this life. What I wanted the most was a house to live in, and we already have that. What else could I wish for? A poor man cannot dream much, son."

"That's where you're getting it wrong, dad!" the boy said, trying to imitate the same tone the teacher had used. "Mr. Raymoney told me that a poor man is not the one without money, but the one without dreams."

The boy told his dad, step by step, everything the teacher had said that day. He explained, in an adult way, that a short-term dream could take up to one year; a medium-term one could take up to ten years; and a long-term dream would take more than ten years to come true.

"Look, son. Up to now, I thought the things this teacher talked about were very reasonable, but this story of not paying the bills to make a dream come true…"

"Dad, he didn't say not to pay the bills. What he said is for you to pay for your dream first, and then the bills."

"What if the money is not enough?"

"That's the part he hasn't taught me yet. He just told me that for the money to be enough you've got to learn how to make a budget, and that's supposed to be tomorrow's lesson."

"All right, all right then. So let's wait until tomorrow to check it out."

"No, dad. You have to think about your dreams today."

Mr. Unaware gave the boy a long stare and thought about how he had grown up and become smart.

"How about your dream, son, what is it?"

"The teacher asked me that today, too, but I only gave him half an answer."

"What do you mean half an answer?"

"It's because I've got two dreams. One of them is not so difficult to make happen. It's just a matter of waiting, as the teacher said."

"What's that dream?"

"My dream is to own a bike. I know it is expensive, dad, but I'll be waiting and saving my allowance. I'm pretty sure of that."

"How about your other dream, son, what is it?"

"My other dream is more difficult, because I don't even know how much it costs."

"Come on, speak up, what is it?"

"My other dream is seeing you making your dream come true and becoming a happier person."

Mr. Unaware was so touched that he couldn't hide the tear that discreetly rolled down his cheek.

"Look, I have another dream in this life that's becoming true right here, right now. I wanted so much to have a good-hearted son that also was a smart boy. And that, I already have. Now this story of yours made me wish for another dream. But, this one I'm not telling you. I promise I'll follow the teachings of your teacher to see if I can make that secret dream happen, too."

That evening Money Boy was feeling blissful. His father was truly interested in his ideas and almost happy. *Yes, my father is almost happy, he thought. What will happen when he's finally able to make one of his dreams come true?*

He went to bed thinking about all the dreams his family could make real from now on. He felt they were as united as ever, and in his heart, he was positive they would have a much better life in the future.

BIKES

Budgeting

Money Boy told the teacher about the talk with his father. He explained his father's uncertainty about saving part of his salary for his dreams.

After listening to what the boy had to say, Mr. Raymoney gave some advice.

"All your father has to do is adjust his budget. A traditional budget is the set of revenues (the money that comes in) and expenditures (the money that goes out). He needs to change the way he is making his budget, inverting the order of priorities. In a DSOP budget, the order is: revenues – dreams = expenditures. Adjusting the budget, in DSOP Methodology, is not about spending less than earning. It means prioritizing dreams and ensuring their accomplishment, reviewing all the expenses (with a diagnosis), and making that dream fit the budget."

"But how, if he keeps saying his money is not enough?"

"Before you receive your allowance, which is a larger sum than what you had before, weren't you able to buy your candy and still keep some coins?"

"Yes."

"Then it means it's always possible to live with less. It's not because you're earning more, that you're going to spend more. Otherwise, your money would be gone."

"That's true," the boy agreed.

"Like I said, the first step is controlling your money better, knowing how it's being spent and changing habits, and saving everything you can. If your father does it, to he'll notice some money left over at the end of the month."

"And what else could he do?"

"He could make better budgets and better purchases. Making budgets also means knowing the price of things. To achieve that, he needs to research prices, visit more than one shop whenever he needs to buy something, and find out the best option. He can make new diagnostics from time to time and identify new opportunities to lower expenses, and make better purchases."

"My mother already does some of that." The boy recalled that he used to go with his mother from supermarket to supermarket to shop for groceries.

"Your mother is a very wise woman. She's been doing many right things, despite not having someone to teach her. However, it's necessary to do that in a more systematic way, comparing prices not once in a while, but always. And you can help both your parents with it, because you're very good at math."

Money Boy was proud.

"Another important tip is to answer some questions very frankly, before going out shopping."

"Which questions are those?" the boy promptly asked.

"For example: "Do I really need that product? Do I have to buy it today? Could I wait a little longer? Do I have all the money to buy it? Does it fit my budget, or am I going to be lacking money for other things?"

"Wow! Many questions, humm?" the boy interrupting the teacher.

"And these are only a few of them," Mr. Raymoney said. "There are many more questions people really should ask before making their shopping decisions. That's what we call conscious consumption."

"What's a conscious person?"

"Being a conscious person is to know what to do and the reason why you do it. Sometimes people act in a certain way, but they don't carefully think through their decisions. If they did, they would make way less mistakes."

"Then I think that's why my mother tells my father to be conscious and change some habits."

"That's for sure! If people were fully conscious of how harmful certain habits are, they probably would change their behavior. It's the same thing with money. If you are a conscious person and know how to give money its real value, you're bound to have a healthier financial life."

The boy was amazed by all the lessons he had learned from Mr. Raymoney. He wished he could speak like that, so easily, about those subjects, so he could teach others everything he had learned. He was still lost in all those thoughts when the teacher added:

"Having a budget is also an important step to make your dreams come true. Do you remember what I told you? That you have to create short-, medium-, and long-term dreams?"

"Yes..." nodded the boy.

"Besides knowing what your dreams are and when you want them to come true, you've also got to know how much they'll cost, to make them fit your budget."

"Ah, I get it," the boy said, trying to remember the price of that bike he had seen at the bike shop.

It appeared as though Mr. Raymoney had read the boy's thoughts.

"For example, let's say your dream is to own a bike. Let's say this bike costs $100 and you want to buy it within ten months. If you save $10 per month, after the tenth month you'll have $100," the teacher said.

"Ah, now I think I got it! If instead of saving $10 per month, I save $20, my dream is going to be real in five months, right?"

The teacher was amazed with the boy's quick thinking. He really was keen to numbers.

"That's it my boy, you've solved the puzzle! And that's true for every dream, short-, medium-, or long-term."

"What if I do the math and the dream doesn't fit my budget? For example, what if I couldn't save $10 a month? Would I have to give up my dream?"

"Giving up? Never! In that case, you would have to extend your term; maybe you'd have to save money during a longer time until you've reached the amount needed."

"Or, cut down the expenses even more," the boy uttered.

"You're indeed an extraordinary kid, you're already thinking on your own. That's exactly it! You'll always be able to make choices. You could, for example, decide not to spend your money on baseball cards and use that money to fulfill your dream."

"That way, there is no dream that cannot be fulfilled, right?"

"It's good you think like that, my boy. Doing so you will achieve anything you want in your life! We're done for today. On Monday, we'll meet again to talk about the last step of the DSOP Methodology. Go home and think over all we've talked about."

As the teacher turned his back, the boy grabbed the notebook and wrote:

1. Learn to live with less than you earn.

2. Save as much as possible.

3. Be a conscious consumer.

4. Make your dreams a priority.

5. Respect your budget.

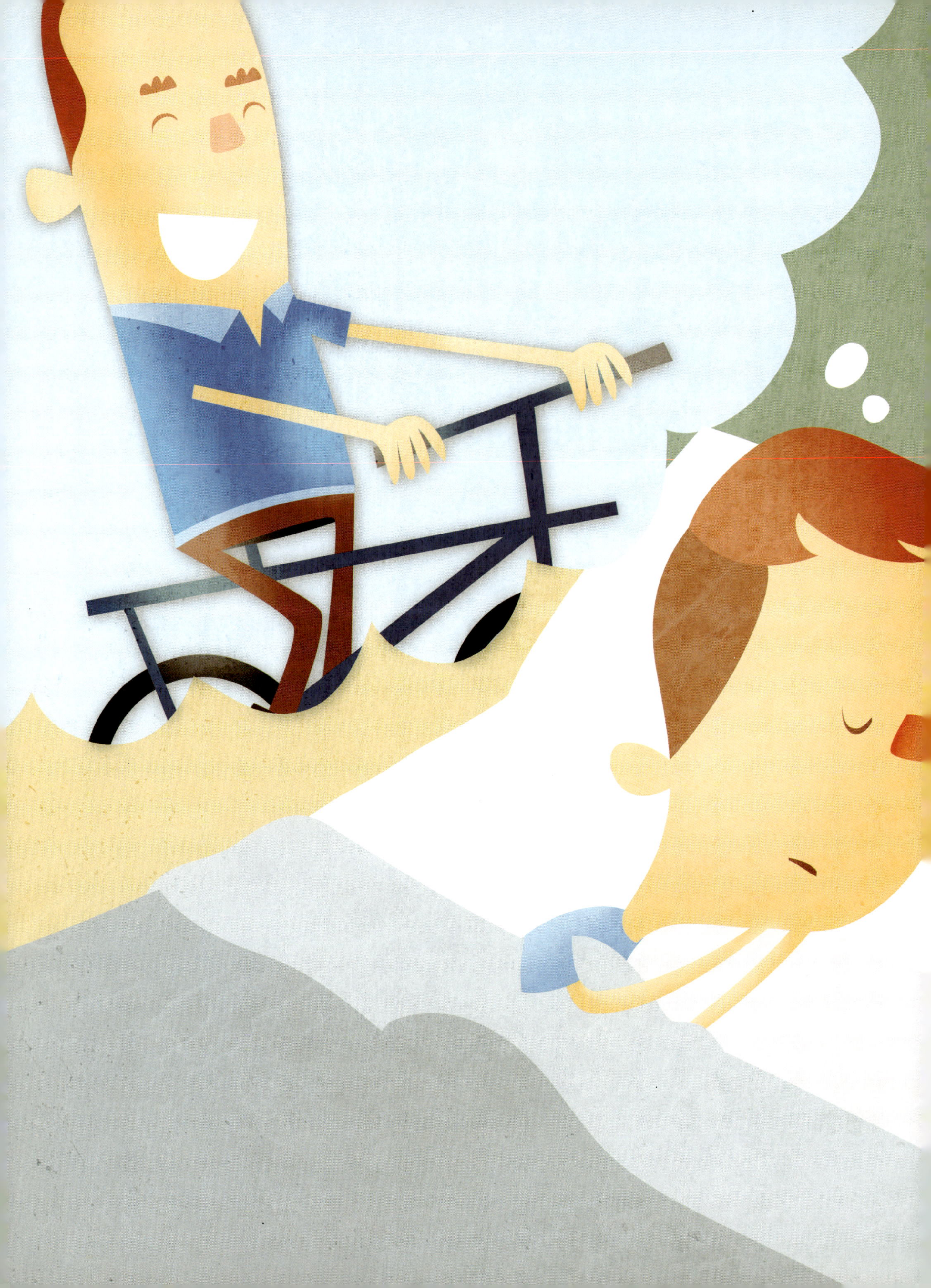

The big secret

In the evening, as it had already become a habit, Money Boy reproduced the conversation he had with Mr. Raymoney to his parents. He explained to them what budgeting was according to the DSOP Methodology, and how important that step was to making dreams happen.

As quickly as he could, Mr. Unaware tried to figure out in his head how much his secret dream would cost; he then told his son.

"Yes, I think that might work. I was here thinking about that dream of mine and I believe if everything goes right, I'll achieve it within five months. I just have to save a little money here and there."

Money Boy was enthusiastic:

"Then tell me daddy, please. What's that dream you have?"

"Oh, son. Now I have to repeat what your mother keeps saying, 'You better wait and be patient, because you'll find out when the time comes.'"

"All right then." the boy said, a little disappointed.

Before he went to his room, Mr. Unaware called him.

"Son, just another thing, are those classes over yet, or is there anything missing?"

"The teacher said there's still one last step, Saving. We'll talk about it on Monday.

"I can hardly wait for Monday to come!" the father said, rubbing his hands.

His reaction made Money Boy get back his good mood at once. He kept staring at his father, intrigued and happy, as he realized he had indeed changed. One thing was still stuck in his head. *What was that dream his father had in mind and insisted in keeping it a secret?*

Mrs. Foresight, who was following the conversation from afar, was also overjoyed to see father and son so close to each other. She was also happy because she realized that the DSOP Methodology was good for her family.

Ever since the first lesson, she had acquired a more accurate overview of her accounts. She had made the diagnosis of how much she earned as a salesperson, and taking daily notes of the money that came in and went out.

She also had chosen three dreams she wanted to come true. Now she had to rethink her dreams doing the math exactly, to figure out how much they would cost. She would like to achieve her short-term dream within a few months. Afterwards, she would have to make that dream fit her budget, just like the teacher advised. That meant improving the savings even more.

That evening Money Boy's home looked like a castle of dreams. Everyone went to bed thinking about what they could achieve by planning for the future, so they could look forward to days of prosperity and joy.

During the night, the boy had a very strange dream in which everything was all mixed up. He woke up frightened, but then he realized he was at home surrounded by his family and he fell back to sleep.

Money Boy - Goes to school

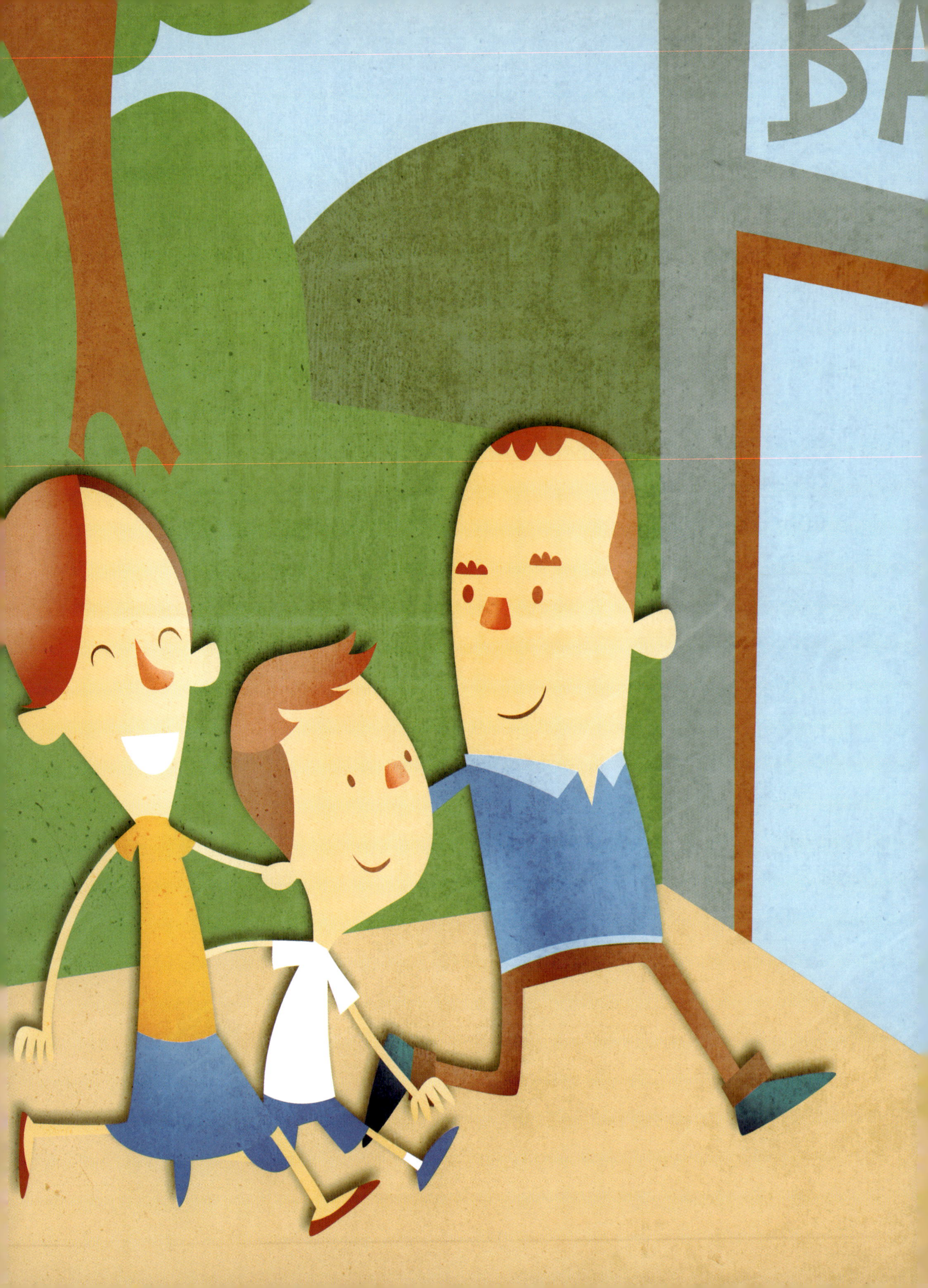

Saving

On a warm summer morning, Money Boy had his last DSOP Methodology lesson with his teacher, Mr. Raymoney.

The teacher asked him to recall everything he had learned. Money Boy described the three first steps of the methodology correctly.

"What could you possibly do to make your dreams come true faster?"

The boy didn't need to think very long to answer.

"Saving more money!"

"That's right! The more you save, the faster your dream will come true. The greater the effort, the less time. There's only one last concept you have to learn."

"And what's that?"

"Saving. Keeping some money, at least a small part of whatever you earn. The more you save, the more you achieve, and faster. This whole process speeds up if you put your money in the bank and gain interest."

"How come?"

"Because you get interest."

"And what's that?"

"It's simply more money. When you have money and keep it in a savings account in a bank, the bank will pay you to keep it there. Each month they will add a little more to what you already have."

"Like they would put some extra coins into the piggy bank?"

"Exactly. Think about the bank as a huge piggy bank, where you put your money every month. The longer your coins are kept there, the more interest they make."

"And what should I do to get this interest?"

"Ask your mother to open a savings account for you. She will go to the bank, deposit your money and leave it there. Whenever you want, you can go to the bank and add some more money. The bank will also add a little each month, which contributes to filling up your piggy faster. When you have enough to make your dream come true, you go to the bank, get the money back and that's it. Your dream is real!"

"That's amazing! Then that's the magic that makes money grow?"

"That's one of the ways to make it grow. There are others, but for now it's enough for you to know how this particular "magic" is made."

"I'm going to ask mom to open a savings account for me today."

"Well done. Money kept at home doesn't produce anything. Besides, you can lose it."

When he heard that, the boy immediately remembered the confusion that had happened with his friend Spender.

"Like when Spender took my wallet?"

"Exactly. I hope you've already forgiven him. Unfortunately, he wasn't lucky enough to have a mother like yours to teach him right. And he's changed a lot since that, hasn't he?"

"Yes he has. We even became friends."

"You see. That's another important teaching for those who want to be financially independent. You need the courage to change behavior and change the way you do things."

Hearing that, Money Boy had an idea.

"I think I'm going to give Spender a piggy bank as a present. Maybe he'll start to save some coins."

"That's an excellent idea!"

"We could also teach him this methodology thing, except he doesn't need it that much, because his father is very rich."

"You're quite wrong. Everyone needs to control their money if they want to live a balanced life. It doesn't matter if you have a little or a lot of money. The important thing is controlling it and using it wisely."

"And dreaming." the boy added.

"Exactly. Because keeping money for the sake of keeping it makes no sense. Keeping money only makes sense if it's for making dreams come true, whether those dreams are yours or other people's dreams. The main thing to have in mind is the fourth and last methodology step, which is Saving"

"Saving means keeping money, right?" Money Boy said.

"That too, but that's not all. People who keep a part of what they earn are saving. But those who control their water, electricity, and telephone usage are saving their money as well."

"That's why my mother keeps telling me not to spend much time in the shower."

"Exactly. Every five minutes you save in the shower, every day, will surely mean a few dollars saved at the end of the month."

The boy was thinking about other things that could help the savings in his home, when Mr. Raymoney began to speak.

"Broadly these are the four steps for those who wish to live a more balanced and happier life. Now that you know all of them, you will be able to put them into practice for everything you wish for in your life and become financially independent. It's very important to repeat the four steps of the methodology at least once a year. After all, as our dreams become a reality, we need to replace them with other dreams and apply the methodology once more.

"Are you saying our classes are over?"

"Yes, this part of the methodology. We'll keep on seeing each other on a daily basis and whenever you have questions, we can talk. Knowledge is something dynamic that changes every single day and needs to be updated frequently."

The boy was becoming sad when the teacher continued.

"From now on, I'd like you to help me spread this methodology to a larger number of people."

"And how can I do that?"

"By teaching the DSOP Methodology first to your parents, then to others."

"I'd love to do that."

"Then from now on you're a multiplier, the boy who will teach everyone financial education through the DSOP Methodology."

The boy happily welcomed that new challenge. After all, everything the teacher had been telling him was making his own life better at home. If only everyone could learn that, too.

"Then that's it, Money Boy. We'll meet again tomorrow in the classroom. If you have any questions, I'll always be around to answer them."

When he arrived home, Money Boy asked his mother to open him a savings account right away.

"Where did you get that idea from, honey?"

"From Mr. Raymoney. He said that besides being safer, the bank is going to pay me for keeping my money there. The more I save, the more I get."

Money Boy anxiously gave Mrs. Foresight an overview of his recent class.

"Seems like a good idea, son."

"Then let's crack my piggy bank!"

"But your birthday is still far from today."

"I know, mom, but the teacher said that money that stays at home won't earn interest."

"Ok, but let's do this. I'll open an account and you can deposit the money that you already have. Every month, when you receive your allowance, you take what you're saving for your dream and we'll deposit that amount, too. The rest you can use for buying your candy and ice cream. Whenever you have some extra coins, they'll go inside the piggy bank. From time to time, we'll go to the bank."

Once again, the boy knew his mother was right, and he was determined to follow her advice.

"Before depositing my money I want to buy two new piggy banks, mom."

"I thought you said you don't want to keep your money at home anymore."

"Yes, but one is for my extra coins, and the other one I want to give to Spender."

"Isn't he the boy that took your money, son?"

"Yes, but we have become friends. I think I forgot to tell you, but the day his dad went to school, I found out that Spender doesn't have a mother."

"Doesn't have a mother? How come?"

"I don't know for sure, but I heard his father talking to the teacher and telling him how hard it is to raise a son without a mother."

Mrs. Foresight thought it over.

"That's right, son. Let's buy your friend a piggy bank. You are doing a very good thing in helping him. Growing up without a mother around must feel awful for a kid. Now go take care of your stuff, I've got to start fixing dinner."

That evening Money Boy gave his father a summary of what his teacher had said that day.

"He told me we've got to put everything into practice and wait for the results to appear. I think everything is going to work out fine," the boy said, waiting for some positive feedback from his father.

"I'd say it's already working fine, son. Your teacher is changing my way of approaching things, and that change is for the better, much better," Mr. Unaware said. "And you better get ready. We're going to the bank, all of us, to open a savings account for each person in this house! Every month we'll be depositing some money to make our dreams come true."

Money Boy - Goes to school

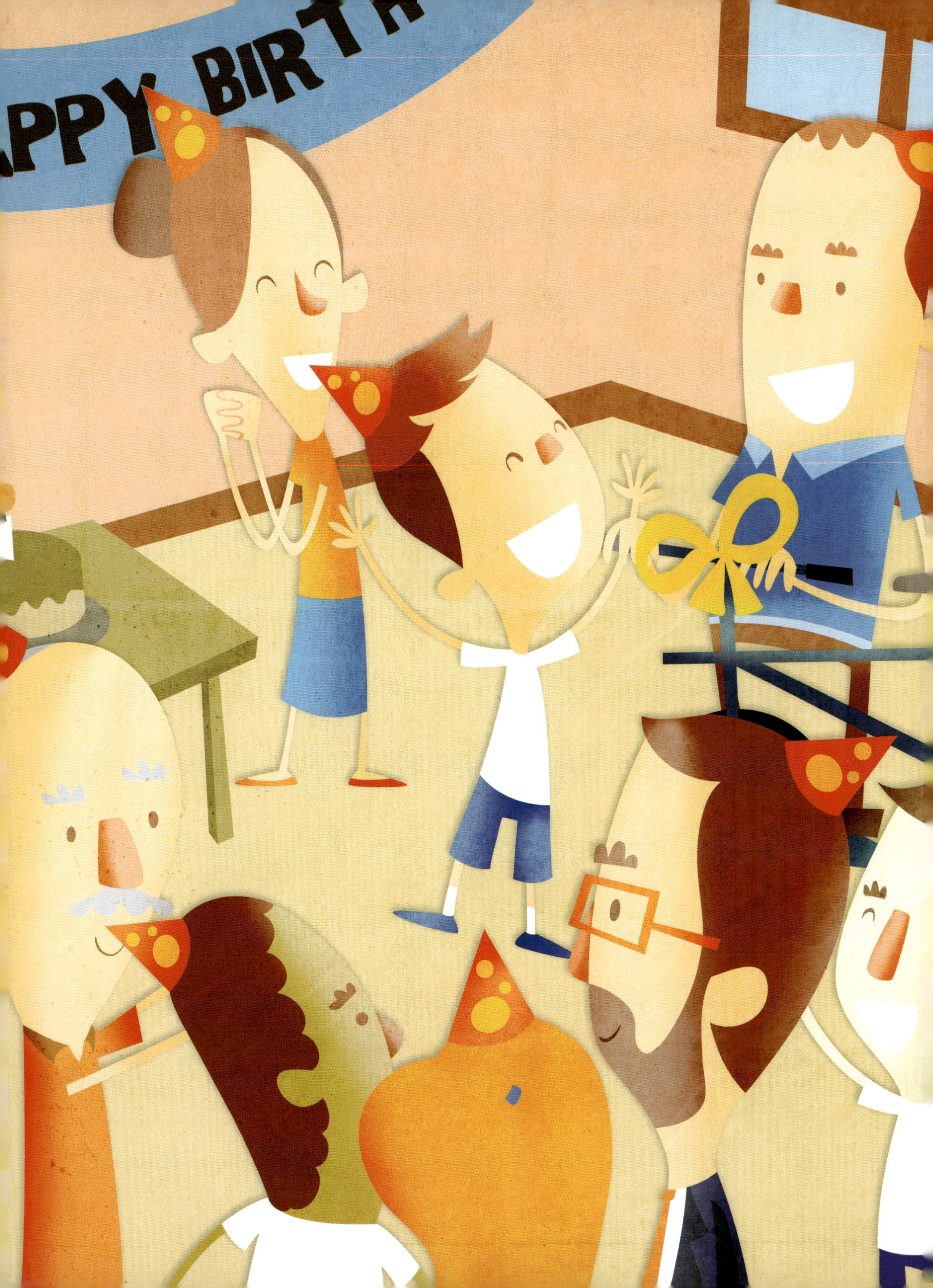
PPY BIRT

A dream never dreamt

That was the year Money Boy was introduced to the DSOP Methodology, and the same year he applied the lessons of Mr. Raymoney to his life and his family.

From time to time, he and his parents would sit together to analyze their expenses and follow up on the progress toward making their dreams come true. However, the boy was the only one to say what his dream was and be clear about it, writing it down on the note pad.

Mrs. Foresight and Mr. Unaware would simply write "dream." It was useless for him to ask what their dreams were, as neither one would say a word.

And so, the months passed by until the year was over. Soon it was school vacation and right after Money Boy's 8th birthday. At that time, he had gathered some money in his savings account, but he didn't even think of spending it. Part of it, he already knew, was reserved for his financial independence. He'd never spend it anyway.

As for his other dreams, as hard as it is to believe it, he wasn't trying to rush into things anymore. He had turned into a patient boy, capable of waiting. He now preferred the safety of money earning interest to the momentary pleasure of small desires.

On his birthday, the boy had one of the greatest surprises of his life. He was already impatient, walking in circles around the house. His mother sent him out to buy some milk at the end of the day, telling him to go to two different stores to compare prices. To do what his mom had asked him took quite some time. When he returned, the house was silent and past the time his daddy should have arrived home.

He opened the kitchen door to a loud roar of voices shouting, "Happy Birthday!" To his surprise, he noticed those voices came from his parents, his classmates, and his teacher, Mr. Raymoney.

A beautiful table set up with a colorful cake, candy, soda and many balloons surrounded all of them. It was his first real birthday party.

He was so overjoyed he didn't see his father leaving and coming back to the room carrying an enormous box wrapped in colorful paper.

With his happiest face ever, Mr. Unaware placed the box in front of Money Boy.

"Here's my birthday present for you, son," giving him a big hug.

Instantly, the boy ripped off the paper and stared at his very first bike.

"My dream, daddy. You gave me my dream! I can't believe it! I can't believe it!"

"No, son. This was my dream that your teacher and the DSOP Methodology helped me achieve."

After that day, the boy made the most important decision of his life: To teach people how to use the DSOP Methodology to make all their dreams come true.

Author
Reinaldo Domingos

www.reinaldodomingos.com.br

Reinaldo Domingos is a master degree, professor, educator, and financial therapist. Author of the books: Financial Therapy; Allowance is not just about money; Get rid of debts; I deserve to have money; Money Boy—family dreams; Money Boy—goes to school; Money Boy—friends helping friends; Money Boy—in a sustainable world; Money Boy—little citizen; Money Boy—time for changes; The Boy and the Money; The Boy, the Money, and the Three Piggy Banks; The Boy, the Money, and the Anthopper; Being wealthy is not a secret; and the series Wealth is not a secret.

In 2009 he created Brazil's first textbook series of financial education aimed at grammar school, already in use by several schools in the country, both private and public. In 2012 he was a pioneer in creating the first financial education program for young apprentices. In 2013 that program also included young adults. In 2014 he created the first financial education course for entrepreneurs, followed by financial education as a university extension course.

Domingos graduated in Accounting and System Analysis. He is the founder of Confirp Accounting and Consulting and was the governor of Rotary International District 4610 (2009-2010). Currently, he is the CEO of DSOP Financial Education and DSOP Publishing. He is the mentor, founder and president of Abef (Brazilian Association of Financial Educators). He is also the creator of Brazil's first postgraduate course in Financial Education and Coaching and mentor of the **DSOP Methodology**.